MW00942719

The Pono
PRINCIPLE

Doing the Right Thing
in All Things

Aloha & Peace,

Robert DeVinck

Robert DeVinck

BALBOA.
PRESS

A DIVISION OF HAY HOUSE

Scriptures taken from the Holy Bible, New International Version®, NIV®. Copyright © 1973, 1978, 1984, 2011 by Biblica, Inc.™ Used by permission of Zondervan. All rights reserved worldwide. www.zondervan.com The "NIV" and "New International Version" are trademarks registered in the United States Patent and Trademark Office by Biblica, Inc.™

Balboa Press books may be ordered through booksellers or by contacting:

Balboa Press
A Division of Hay House
1663 Liberty Drive
Bloomington, IN 47403
www.balboapress.com
1 (877) 407-4847

Because of the dynamic nature of the Internet, any web addresses or links contained in this book may have changed since publication and may no longer be valid. The views expressed in this work are solely those of the author and do not necessarily reflect the views of the publisher, and the publisher hereby disclaims any responsibility for them.

The author of this book does not dispense medical advice or prescribe the use of any technique as a form of treatment for physical, emotional, or medical problems without the advice of a physician, either directly or indirectly. The intent of the author is only to offer information of a general nature to help you in your quest for emotional and spiritual well-being. In the event you use any of the information in this book for yourself, which is your constitutional right, the author and the publisher assume no responsibility for your actions.

Any people depicted in stock imagery provided by Thinkstock are models, and such images are being used for illustrative purposes only. Certain stock imagery © Thinkstock.

Print information available on the last page.

ISBN: 978-1-5043-9222-8 (sc)
ISBN: 978-1-5043-9223-5 (hc)
ISBN: 978-1-5043-9301-0 (e)

Library of Congress Control Number: 2017918024

Balboa Press rev. date: 11/22/2017

To my father, Walter, who taught me pono by living it, and to my mother, Johanna, whose dying wish was for me to write because she believed "there is greatness there."

When in innocency, or when by intellectual perception, he attains to say, - 'I love the Right; Truth is beautiful within and without, forevermore. Virtue, I am thine: save me: use me: thee I will serve, day and night, in great, in small, that I may be not virtuous, but virtue;' - then is the end of the creation answered, and God is well pleased.

- Ralph Waldo Emerson

Contents

Preface xi

Introduction.. xiii

Chapter 1   What Is Pono? 1
Chapter 2   Doing The Next Right Thing.............. 13
Chapter 3   Who Am I, Really? 25
Chapter 4   Pono In Recovery.............................. 39
Chapter 5   Pono In The Workplace 53
Chapter 6   Pono In Politics................................. 67
Chapter 7   Pono And The Environment................ 79
Chapter 8   Living Pono 91
Chapter 9   Eating Pono 105
Chapter 10   Being Pono 119

Afterword.. 131
Acknowledgments 133
Endnotes... 135
About the Author 139

Preface

My father taught me *pono*. More accurately, my father demonstrated *pono* throughout his life - he lived *pono*. Although he may never have seen the Hawaiian word in print, or heard it spoken, nonetheless he practiced *pono* in everything he did. You see, my father always believed in doing the right thing, and only now, many years after his death, do I realize how much he personified the true definition of the word.

But what is the true definition of *pono?* In the definitive and authoritative Pukui & Elbert *Hawaiian Dictionary* (1986), one finds:

> *pono. 1. nvs. Goodness, uprightness, morality, moral qualities, correct or proper procedure, excellence, well-being, prosperity, welfare, benefit, behalf, equity, sake, true condition or nature, duty; moral, fitting, proper, righteous, right, upright, just, virtuous, fair, beneficial, successful, in perfect order, accurate, correct, eased, relieved; should, ought, must, necessary.[1]*

Out of those 35 different definitions, representing a multitude of assorted contexts, most Hawaiians would tell you that the most common usage of the word *pono* is when defining someone who is righteous, or an act of righteousness (as used in the Hawaii state motto: *Ua Mau ke Ea o ka 'Āina i ka Pono* or *The life of the land is perpetuated in righteousness).* There are also many Hawaiians who interpret *living pono* as a spiritual way of life, often with regards to how one treats other people, and the *'āina* (land). I wish to be very clear that this book, *The Pono Principle,* is neither an attempt to delve into the multiplicity of uses of the word *pono,* nor to approach the term from a Hawaiian cultural perspective only.

For the purpose of this book, I will be using the word *pono* in its most common usage - the act of doing the right thing. Since this honorable act is a universal virtue, one that transcends all cultures, countries, religions, and languages, I will, henceforth, refrain from italicizing the word pono. This noble word, although of Hawaiian birth, deserves to become part of the entire world's everyday lexicon. Never again should the word pono sound "foreign" to anyone, anymore than the practice of its principle, about which this book is written.

The Pono Principle represents how immeasurably our lives can be impacted, and transformed, simply by the daily practice of doing the right thing *in all things*. What follows is a glimpse of the many life lessons I've learned by living, eating, and being pono. It is also a chronicle of how much more wonderful life can be when one's guiding principle is pono.

Mahalo nui loa, Dad

Your loving, and grateful, son,

Robert DeVinck

Maui, Hawaii

Introduction

(The Legend of Pono)

Once upon a dream, when time was new, there was a remote tropical island where the first two people were created. Their names were Keoni and Luana and everything they knew as truth they learned from the world around them – the sea, the sky, the land, and each other. What they learned from those life sources determined how they thought, and how they acted.

Keoni and Luana loved to sit on the pristine crescent beach and observe the waves breaking on the shore. They especially loved the dawn of day when they could watch the bright orange halo in the sky rise from the ocean, ascending towards the heavenly clouds of pink and purple hues. Keoni and Luana often walked through the lush fern and bamboo rainforest, holding hands, as they followed the cool streams that were lined with fragrant, colorful flowers. The streams would lead them to a number of tranquil pools that lay beneath the cascading waterfall that poured down the side of the mountain.

Coconuts taught Keoni many life lessons. The very first time that Keoni broke open a fallen coconut with a rock, he discovered several things – the water inside the coconut was very refreshing, the meat tasted good, and when one fell on his head, it hurt. He showed Luana how to eat and drink from the coconut, and that made her smile. After eating all of the fallen coconuts lying about, Keoni figured out that, if he wanted more coconuts, he would have to climb the trees to get them. Many times, Keoni fell from the trees and many times his feet were cut from his attempts.

Over time, Keoni became quite adept at climbing coconut trees, but he still cut his feet with every attempt. One day, Luana wrapped his feet with ti leaves and tied them to his ankles by weaving ti leaves into strands. This worked very well, and Keoni never cut his feet again climbing coconut trees. Every time he would tie the ti leaves to his feet, before ascending a coconut tree, he would think about Luana and smile.

After many months of eating coconuts, and discarding the shells all along the beach, both Keoni and Luana noticed that the beach did not appear as beautiful as they remembered it once being. So they decided to pick up all of the discarded coconut shells and toss them into a cave. In the mornings that followed, as the orange halo rose from the ocean, they looked upon their spotless beach and witnessed the fruitful results of their efforts.

Keoni and Luana discovered a wide variety of other food sources from the many fruit trees and vegetables that grew on the island. Everything they needed to survive surrounded them in abundance. Using strands of fiber from the coconuts, Keoni made rope and, from the rainforest, he obtained bamboo. Using the bamboo and coconut rope, Keoni and Luana built a house within the vast canopy of the largest tree near the beach.

One day, when Keoni and Luana were walking along the beach, they saw a giant creature of the sea washed up on the shore. Slowly they approached, marveling at the shear size of something that they had only seen, from a distance, leaping out of the ocean with grace and majesty. Standing next to the enormous sea creature made Keoni and Luana feel very small and meek.

Keoni and Luana felt completely connected to the world around them. Everything they observed and experienced became their truth. Their shared experience, their mutual consciousness, taught them that they were only part of something much bigger than themselves. From observing the small sea creatures with shells on their backs and bellies, Keoni learned how to swim underwater and to come up for air when necessary. From listening to the creatures of the sky, which lived in the trees, Luana learned how to sing. They were truly one with the beautiful world around them.

Over a period of time Luana's tummy started to grow, and it

kept growing. And then she began to feel something moving inside of her. Keoni was concerned for Luana and stayed close by her side. On a beautiful starlit night, with the sound of the waves crashing upon the shore, Luana gave birth to a baby girl. In the twilight of morning, Keoni brought the baby to the water's edge and held her up towards the sea and sky, naming her Kailani. Following the birth of their little girl, Keoni and Luana discovered a newfound joy in their lives, and their hearts were filled with gratitude.

As she grew, Kailani was taught everything that her parents had learned from observing the world around them. Mostly, she learned by watching their example. And, because Kailani was such an observant and intelligent girl herself, she learned some new things that her parents had never taught her. She learned the songs of the giant sea creatures and could anticipate when they would return to the island. She also learned how to cultivate the land, transplanting fruit-bearing trees from other parts of the island so that her family would have easily accessible food.

The greatest life lesson that Kailani learned from her parents was love. As she grew, she accepted the truth that love embodied all that she observed around her. Love was in her parents' smiles, love was in the song of the soaring sky creatures, love was in the food that the island provided to her family, love was in her mother's preparation of that food, and love is what filled their tree house that overlooked the crescent beach where they lived.

More than anything, Kailani knew that love was always the right thing. She knew that truth in her mind, in her heart, and in her soul. Love was never wrong. By observing how her parents treated each other, how they respected and cared for the land, and how they stood in awesome wonder at the sight of a star-filled night sky, Kailani knew that love surrounded them and that it was right. And so she named what is right, and the act of doing what is right, Pono. In all things, and in all ways, being pono became her family's guiding principle. Kailani's family demonstrated pono in how they loved and honored each other, the island, and all creatures, big and small. And everything in the world was better because of it.

The Common Good

Chapter 1

What Is Pono?

Pono is the life, that wonderful life, you were meant to live.
- Ka'ala Souza

Doubt what you will, but let us never forget what is right. In every civilized society since the genesis of the human race, it has been considered wrong for a person to physically assault others, to steal from them, or to harm them in any way. There are laws that exist to protect persons from such behavior (which we call *crimes*), and laws to punish those who wish to do such harm to others (whom we call *criminals*). A good society attempts to legislate such that it helps protect its citizens from being victims of such wrong, criminal behavior but also to habituate its citizens to act virtuously. But putting civil laws aside, don't people already have some kind of learned sense of what wrong behavior looks like and feels like? And if they do, then don't they also understand what doing the right thing feels and looks like?

I believe that all of us internally possess a sense of what is right and wrong. It is out of this common sense (that which has been shared by the majority of humanity throughout history) that individuals find it possible to coexist in an otherwise chaotic world. But just being well versed in what constitutes *thou shalt not* behavior doesn't mean that the majority of people spend much time concentrating on doing what is right. *The Pono Principle* is the paradigm that makes that focal shift happen.

So many of our day-to-day decisions are based primarily on what needs to be done in the moment, with little (if any) thought to whether such decisions are for the betterment of our lives, let alone for the rest of the world. I will demonstrate how simply tweaking our decision-making process - by asking ourselves what is the right thing to do in this situation - can transform our lives forever. Should I eat a healthy salad for lunch, or a burger and fries from a fast-food restaurant? Should I exercise today, or skip it? Should I get in the habit of saying "good morning" to people I pass on the street, or simply ignore them? Should I pick up that wrapper on the floor, or assume that someone else will?

It is important for you, the reader, to understand that this book is not intended to tell you, or even suggest to you, what you should for shouldn't do in life. As pointed out by Louise Hay in *You Can Heal Your Life* (1984), the inference in using the word *should* is that you are doing something wrong. Therefore, I would advise the reader to stop asking questions with the word *should* and substitute the word *could* in its place. *Could* I eat a healthier lunch than what is offered at that fast-food restaurant? *Could* I make time to exercise sometime today? *Could* I develop the habit of saying "good morning" to people I pass by? *Could* I be mindful to start picking up litter when I see it? As Joyce so eloquently reminds us, "Could gives us choice, and we are never wrong."[2]

Most people will say, "I already know that I should (or better yet, could) eat healthier, exercise, and be nicer to other people and the environment." Are you actually *doing* those things? Knowing what is right is a far cry from doing what is right, and *The Pono Principle* is your guidebook on how to act on what you already know to be the next right thing to do.

Live and Learn

We learn by observing the world around us, by attempting to understand what we observe, and by remembering those observations. What we refer to as *life lessons* are those mental, physical, and spiritual observations we have made over a lifetime, observations that have taught us something - a truth, a feeling, a belief. As humans, the gamut of life lessons runs from learning how to take our first steps by holding onto our parents' hands, to learning how to take our last steps by holding onto a cane or walker.

Part of augmenting our own learning curve is to witness how other living creatures learn. As a member of an outrigger canoe club on the island of Maui, I have been blessed many times in being able to closely observe the natural wonder of the seasonal migration of the great humpback whales. To witness firsthand a mother whale teaching her newborn calf how to swim, eat, and navigate the ocean is a transcendent experience. To submerge into their underwater world, and to hear the humpback mating and feeding songs being communicated through miles of ocean, is to witness the innate ability of these graceful leviathans of the deep to both understand and react to the message of these songs.

Through a combination of natural instinct and learned behavior, all animals (including humans) evolve, reacting to their environment according to what they know both instinctively and from observation. Oftentimes, trial and error adds a new dimension to the life lessons we learn. Teaching a child not to touch a hot stove may fall on deaf ears until the child burns his or her finger for the first time, only then understanding that the parental warning was not just empty words but sound advice.

But what we learn in life, about ourselves and the world around us, does not define us as people. The mass accumulation of life lessons over many years only amounts to an encyclopedic measure of knowledge, nothing more. That is to say, *what we know* (or even how much we know) has little, if anything, to do with *who we are.* The fact that someone can recite the Ten Commandments verbatim, for example, is a far different thing from someone choosing to implement them as a moral compass to live by. The true measure of a person can only be determined by *how we act,* based on the life lessons we have learned.

Walk the Talk

For about forty years of my mortal existence, I spent an awful lot of time talking about wanting to be a writer and even more time actually referring to myself as a writer. What was missing from both the former aspiration and the latter self-image was something called a completed book. The fact that you are at this very moment reading these words, while holding this book with my name on its cover and spine, demonstrates that I have just now earned the right to call myself a writer (and a published writer at that).

Some years ago, at a writer's symposium I attended in Washington State, I heard author J. A. Jance give what I believe to be the best definition of a writer: "A writer is someone who has written something today." Boy, that definition shortened the long list of self-proclaimed writers to a precious few. What Jance so boldly stated with her punch-to-the-solar-plexus reality check was that writers write. They don't talk about writing; they write.

In like fashion, for every person who has ever earned a college degree, there are thousands of others who have only thought about getting their degrees but didn't. People who wanted to learn how to play a musical instrument but didn't. People who only thought about reading *War and Peace* but never did. The only difference between these types of people and the college graduates, guitar players, and the *War and Peace* readers lies in their inability to act on their passive intentions. College graduates apply to colleges and study hard for four years to attain their degrees, guitar players buy a guitar and practice for years to learn their craft, and *War and Peace* readers simply take the time to read a classic work of literature one page at a time. One group talks about doing something, while the other is already out there *doing it.*

Taking action is the key to accomplishing anything. I can't think of any goal in life that doesn't incorporate action steps. Someone desirous of getting from the living room couch to the kitchen refrigerator, for example, cannot accomplish that goal without taking a certain number of steps (physical ones) to get there. So it is with every other desired outcome in life, whether physical, mental, or spiritual. To act is to do.

Follow Your Conscience

Now that we have progressed from thought to action and are actually doing something, what is it that we could be focused on doing? Well, how about doing something that will benefit or improve our personal lives? Better yet, how about acting in a way that will benefit those around us, thus improving our world? Now we're on to something.

The sooner we as people learn that our actions do not exist in a bubble - that everything we do in life (in some measure) affects other people - the sooner we will act in a manner that adds consciousness to the equation. Whether that conscious thought takes the form of social consideration, a sense of morality, or just a feeling in our gut, the action that follows will be rooted in doing what we perceive to be the right thing to do.

Let's take a simple occurrence, like staying at a hotel, to see how other people and our environment could possibly be affected by the personal choices we make as hotel guests. Due to a desire to conserve energy, many hotels today offer their guests the option to go green during their stay. What that means is that guests can choose to reduce or refuse housekeeping service by reusing towels more than once and by not having sheets changed or rooms vacuumed every single day. Because I often travel alone, I always refuse housekeeping altogether. Usually I am rewarded for going green by being given additional hotel reward points, or a $5 restaurant coupon, for every day that I refuse housekeeping service.

When you think about the amount of manpower, water, and energy it takes just to do the laundry in a major hotel, and how easy it is to help cut down on the wasting of those precious resources, how can we consciously not choose to do what's pono? You talk about how one socially conscious decision (i.e. to go green when you stay at a hotel) can benefit you, others, and the environment - all at one time - there it is. Although it is only one example of doing the right thing for the common good, it is a very positive way to demonstrate the classic win-win-win dynamic known as *The Pono Principle.*

The ABCs of *Pono*

Not wishing to get into a huge philosophical discussion on the subject of morality and ethics, I am about to make one very broad assumption about you, the reader. Whether I am correct in this assumption only God knows, but I am willing to bet that you and I share a common sense of morality, a common belief in what is right and wrong. Regardless of our differences in race, gender, nationality, political views, or ethnic background, I am confident that the vast majority of us navigate through life sharing a common moral compass.

To make my point I have chosen three very influential historical figures who not only shared, but also preached the benefits of, a common belief that doing the right thing (i.e. pono) should be central to our existence. All three of these men lived over two thousand years ago and their truths are as relevant today as at any other time in human history. Here is a short primer of their basic pono teachings.

"A" is for Aristotle

In *Book II* of the *Nicomachean Ethics,*[3] Aristotle posits that the person who possesses moral virtue or excellence of character does the right thing in all things, discerning the right means to the right end. Moral virtue *(aretê)* is the active condition of the soul that makes someone consistently choose the right action to take. According to Aristotle, a person develops this ability based on a combination of his upbringing and his character *(êthos)*. Virtue of thought comes about through teaching, while virtue of character is brought out through habit and constant practice. Although humans may not be *born virtuous,* Aristotle writes, we *are* all born with the capacity to be morally virtuous, and it is only by behaving in the right way that we train ourselves to be virtuous. And the earlier in life that we can begin the habit of practicing virtuous behavior (what I call *The Pono Principle),* the better for all of us and our world.

Moral virtues happen because of habits. The virtue of a man is the habit from which he becomes good. According to Aristotle, moral virtue is best displayed by the "decent person" *(epieikês),* the person who recognizes and chooses to do the right thing. It is in human decency that he finds the best example of human goodness. And it is in human decency where we find the morally virtuous, the beautiful, and the good. It is where we find pono.

"B" is for Buddha

There are Four Noble Truths at the heart of Buddhist teaching. Once we have acknowledged that we suffer (The First Noble Truth), we then must identify the roots of our suffering (The Second Noble Truth). When we cease to do the things that make us suffer, we have attained The Third Noble Truth. But it is The Fourth Noble Truth, called the Noble Eightfold Path, which holds the answer to our future. It is the path that leads to our transformation from suffering to well-being. The Eight Paths are: Right View, Right Thinking, Right Speech, Right Action, Right Livelihood, Right Diligence, Right Mindfulness, and Right Concentration.

Knowing that the Hawaiian word for *right* is pono, it is certainly no leap to suggest that if Buddha had been from Hawaii, his entire Noble Eightfold Path would have been called "The Pono Way." In the same way that I define *The Pono Principle* as being beneficial to ourselves, others, and the world around us, Buddha also viewed the Eightfold Path as "the right way" for us to practice actions that are both personally and mutually beneficial. When we are mindful of our actions, when we know that our intentions are good and that our actions will be helpful to everyone, Buddha says, that's when we know when something is right or wrong.

"C" is for Christ

Jesus Christ is the ultimate example of a life dedicated to always doing the right thing. Those who observed his actions firsthand witnessed humility, compassion, love, tolerance and forgiveness on a level never before seen. Jesus' entire life was a moral template for all to follow. He lived his life in obedience to his Father, and he brought hope and light to everyone he encountered. His primary message was one of love. By emphasizing God's unconditional love for us, Jesus asked only one thing in return – that we love God and love our neighbor. According to Jesus, love is not only the right thing to do – it is actually the only thing to do. So it is with pono.

It is because of God's love for us, and our love for Him and others, that we feel compelled to want to follow Jesus' example of always doing the right thing. We accomplish that, as Jesus did, by loving and serving others. That's the pono way. The most profound transformation one can experience is to *become* the one who washes the feet of others, and dries them with the towel wrapped around one's waist. The sole purpose of *The Pono Principle* is to help guide you toward that transformation.

Of course, Jesus also spoke a great deal about Peace. In fact, He uses the word *peace* over 100 times in the Bible. In the Old Testament, Isaiah prophesized the birth of Jesus by referring to Him as the Prince of Peace. Christians believe that knowing the Prince of Peace (i.e. accepting Jesus as the Son of God), allows them to not only possess eternal peace with God but to also experience a peace in their hearts that transcends all human understanding.

The fulfillment of that promise comes from living a life of pono which I will illustrate using (what I refer to as) *The Pono Prayer*.

The Pono Prayer

I can think of no better example of a Pono Prayer than that of St. Paul's final exhortations in his letter to the people of Philippi (circa 62 AD). The first verse (Philippians 4:8 New International Version) concerns *right thinking* - on what "things" our thoughts should be focused on:

> *Whatever is true, whatever is noble, whatever is right, whatever is pure, whatever is lovely, whatever is admirable—if anything is excellent or praiseworthy— think about such things.*[4]

But thoughts without actions, as previously discussed, is not enough to live a fulfilled life. The second verse (Phil. 4:9 NIV) reminds us that *thinking* about "whatever is right" is only the first step. In this verse, St. Paul teaches us that *right living* (i.e. living pono) can only be achieved when we take our *right thinking* and "put it into practice":

> *Whatever you have learned or received or heard from me, or seen in me - put it into practice. And the God of peace will be with you.*[5]

And the reward for *right thinking* and *right living*, according to St. Paul? Nothing short of the promise that "the God of peace will be with you."

A Pono Life Lesson

A married couple goes to the local hardware store to buy two canoe paddles. The husband chooses a bent shaft paddle and his wife chooses a straight shaft paddle (which is $10 less in price). After picking up a few other supplies they proceed to the front of the store to pay for their items. As they approach the cashier station the young girl behind the counter appears to be fighting a head cold and is wiping her nose with a tissue. The husband's first instinct is to cower from the cashier for fear of catching her cold. He is somewhat relieved when he sees her squirt some sanitizer onto her hands before she touches the items they are purchasing. He asks her if she is sick and she just nods in the affirmative.

Not noticing that there is a $10 difference in price between the two paddles the couple are buying, the cashier begins to ring up the paddles by charging them the lesser amount times two. When the wife notices that her husband's paddle is priced $10 more than hers, she brings it to the cashier's attention who thanks her for her honesty. As the couple grabs their supplies to leave, the wife says to the cashier that she hopes that she feels better soon. The cashier smiles and wishes both of them a good day.

Here's the point: The husband was prepared to allow the cashier to charge them the same price for the two paddles (even though he knew that his paddle was priced $10 more than the other). He even cringed a little when his wife brought this fact to the cashier's attention. Had the wife not said anything, the husband was ready to pay the lesser amount, and then run for the parking lot before the cashier caught her mistake. He also showed no empathy for the fact that the cashier was fighting a cold. His only concern was that he might possibly catch her germs.

How many times have we taken advantage of employee mistakes when it comes to undercharging us on a bill, or overpaying us when they hand us our change? Whether it's a waiter who forgets to charge us for that second bottle of wine, or a bank cashier who gives us an extra $20 bill by mistake, we are thieves for not bringing the mistake to their attention *in the moment,* not days later (after our consciences compel us to).

As the author of this book, dealing with the subject matter of doing the right thing, I am embarrassed to admit to you, the reader, that I was the husband in the example above and my wife was the honest woman in the story. The event occurred exactly as I have written it. When we returned home, I not only thought about my actions at the hardware store, but also of my wife's. That night as we were lying in bed, I confessed to her my thoughts from earlier that day, and thanked her for being an inspiration to me for doing the right thing. You see, practicing *The Pono Principle* in one's day-to-day life is an ongoing challenge - for *all* of us.

Pono in Action

Chapter 2

Doing The Next Right Thing

The truth of the matter is that you always know the
right thing to do. The hard part is doing it.
- Robert H. Schuller

Now that we understand that we share a common sense of what is the right thing to do, the challenging part it would seem is in *doing* it. This is where I will suggest to the reader how to take simple action steps by applying *The Pono Principle* to their daily "to do" list. You see - pono, in and of itself, is the secret ingredient to getting things done.

I will assume that most people do not believe that the vast majority of their day-to-day decisions set the world on fire. After all, the only people who truly benefit from your decision to eat a burger and fries at a local fast-food restaurant are the owners and stockholders of that fast-food chain. They certainly don't know you personally and therefore could care less about your cholesterol levels, blood pressure, or susceptibility to diabetes caused by your personal eating habits. But when you make a conscious decision to eat a salad made with only organically grown ingredients, you have not only empowered yourself physically, but you have also helped local farmers and the environment. You have also made a conscious decision not to harm, yet alone kill, any animals in the process. That is called a collective win, or what is more commonly referred to as a "win-win situation." Because of the threefold benefit of pono (i.e. I win, we win, and the world wins), by using *The Pono Principle* in making decisions, one will find that the vast majority of outcomes are, by definition, not just a "win-win" situation, but almost always a "win-win-win" situation.

When people begin to experience more positive outcomes resulting from their decisions to frame their actions on what is pono (i.e. right), then applying *The Pono Principle* to their lives becomes not only more habitual, but also more motivating. Doing the right thing will become second nature to us. Practicing pono in all that we do, while seeing the mutually beneficial results of our actions, motivates us to continue thinking and acting in this new way – the way of pono.

My mother used to tell me that, when I was a baby, she would often look at my tiny feet and try to imagine all of the roads that those feet would take me down over the course of my lifetime. I would oftentimes remember her words as I was lacing up my Army boots before going out on maneuvers, or walking with my wife on a white sand beach in Bora Bora, or dancing with my daughters on their wedding days. The steps that I have taken on my life journey have brought me here – to a place where I have the privilege to share with you steps that might also lead you to a more purposeful life. Again, what follows is what worked for me. I can only suggest that *The Pono Principle* could very well work for you, too.

A One-Step Program

The vast majority of self-help and motivational programs contain a set of multiple action steps that need to be accomplished in order to attain one's personal and/or business goals. The unique quality of *The Pono Principle* is that there is really only one step necessary to completely transform your life – just do the next right thing. That bears repeating. If you want to maximize the amount of good that you can do for yourself, others, and the world in which we live, then the surest and most effective way for you to accomplish that goal is to *do the next right thing.*

Stop and think about it. God gave Moses Ten Commandments so that the human race could have a set of laws to instruct them on what they should and shouldn't do to please God. It was also a means to help the human race coexist in a more peaceful environment than what they had experienced prior to that time. Some think of the Ten Commandments as mankind's moral compass; certainly for Judeo-Christians they are. But in purely layman's terms aren't the Ten Commandments, Buddha's Noble Eightfold Path, and The Twelve Step Program (just to name a few) all examples of pono action steps? Whether you want to think of them as mere suggestions (12 Steps), spiritual guidelines (Eightfold Path), or rules to obey (10 Commandments), they all are intended to help individuals do the right thing.

In a way, what *The Pono Principle* is designed to do is to distill the moral wisdom of the ages down to a single act – what you are doing at this very moment. Obviously, you are reading a book about Pono, which, by definition, is the right thing to do. What a great starting point, right? My genuine hope is that you continue to read as long as possible. But at some point you will need to bookmark where you left off reading so that you may move on to your next activity. *The Pono Principle* will help you do that next right thing, whether it's answering the doorbell (with a smile and a "good morning"), preparing yourself a (healthy) breakfast, or heading off to your job (which provides the income to support you and your family). Whatever the next thing is on your daily "to do" list, just make sure that it is pono. What you will find, by consciously performing these positive action steps, is that they are a far cry from the everyday, mundane decisions you used to make when just *doing* seemed to be enough.

So, where do we begin? Before you can do the *next* right thing, you might want to start with one fundamental right thing upon which to build. How about *love?* Better yet, how about *selfless love?* God commands it. I highly recommend it.

Selfless Love, the Greatest Commandment

In Mark 12:28-31, Jesus is in the temple in Jerusalem, speaking to the chief priests, the scribes, and the elders. These very threatened religious men are doing all they can to try to entrap Jesus so as to have him arrested. But they are no match for his superior scriptural knowledge, intellect, and reasoning. Frustrated, many of them leave the temple, but a lone scribe approaches Jesus to ask a question about the Commandments; specifically, whether there was one which Jesus would identify as being the most important.

> *One of the teachers of the law came and heard them debating. Noticing that Jesus had given them a good answer, he asked him, 'Of all the commandments, which is the most important?'*

> *'The most important one, answered Jesus, is this: 'Hear, O Israel: The Lord our God, the Lord is one. Love the Lord your God with all your heart and with all your soul and with all your mind and with all your strength.' The second is this: 'Love your neighbor as yourself.' There is no commandment greater than these.[6]*

Like all Jews of his time, the scribe understood that God's Law was inscribed on the Ten Commandments - *Ten* Commandments - not Eight, not Four, and not Two. But the scribe is like the overweight man who is told by his doctor that, in order to get in shape, he has to eat a healthy diet every day, and exercise regularly. Instead, he wants to know if there are one or two prescription pills he can take (in lieu of dieting and exercising) to achieve the weight loss he desires. In other words, the scribe doesn't want to do the hard work of following God's long list of *Ten* Commandments if there is an easier way to go (i.e. a shorter list).

Jesus sees through the scribe, so He *prescribes* to him a "two pill" alternative: "Love the Lord your God" and "Love your neighbor." No doubt, the scribe must have felt like someone given a commuted sentence of sorts, or the secret to a shortcut to Heaven. To his ears, what he probably heard Jesus say to him was, "If Ten Commandments are too much for you to handle, just focus on these Two and you'll be fine." I can only imagine the scribe's elation at thinking that his "to do" list from God had just been reduced by 80%.

Here lies the (dare I say) shrewdness of Jesus. What must have sounded like a paring down of the Ten Commandments to only Two was, in truth, merely a consolidation of all of them into Two. What Jesus did was consolidate the religious imperatives of the first Three Commandments (i.e. not having other gods, not taking the Lord's name in vain, and remembering the Sabbath) under the aggregate directive "Love the Lord your God," while consolidating the moral imperatives of the last Seven Commandments (i.e. honoring your parents, not murdering, committing adultery, stealing, bearing false witness, coveting your neighbor's wife, nor his goods) under "Love your neighbor." Thus, Jesus basically synthesized in Two very generic Commandments what His Father stipulated in Ten very specific ones.

But the real discovery of truth in what Jesus says, found in the one common word shared in both Commandments, is that He tells us to do one thing – love. He commands us to love. Since Jesus knows that we already suffer from an egocentric love of ourselves, He commands us to love others as much. But it is a *selfless* love that Jesus is talking about. He commands us to love God, and to love our neighbor. That's it. Lesson's over. The chief priests, the scribes, and the elders are hereby dismissed. "And from then on no one dared ask him any more questions"[7] (Mark 12:34 NIV).

Pono Reading

Let's take a look at what we choose to read. The fact that you have chosen my book to read at this moment, as opposed to a multitude of other options, warms my heart. It never ceases to amaze

18

me how many people I see on airplanes, or lying on the beach, reading whatever suspense or romance novel today's bestselling *auteur du jour* has written. From time to time I will ask someone why they choose to read that particular genre of book, and the answer is always the same: "I don't want to have to think too much while I'm reading on vacation." I'm sorry but, personally, I find that reason to be a complete waste of valuable reading time. Mind you, that's just my opinion.

In the same vein as those who would argue that "Life is too short to drink cheap wine," I would offer, "Life is too short to read mindless books." After all, there are only so many hours in the day, and only so many days in one's life, and if I'm going to spend those precious hours reading, you better believe I will choose to read something like *The Great Gatsby* long before reading a book where "I don't have to think too much." I used to read in bed just before going to sleep but, more times than not, I would doze off and not remember what I read when I awoke in the morning. Today, I choose to reserve an hour, each and every morning, to read from the multitude of books lying next to me. At the very least, I read from a half dozen daily meditation books, a classic work of fiction, a biography, a spiritual work, and a self-help book. I choose to read these books, and others like them, precisely for the reason that they *are* mindful (not mindless) sources of inspiration. They are what I would refer to as pono reading material.

Don't get me wrong. From time to time, I still love to read a good history book or a well-crafted collection of essays. But to maximize the personal benefits I receive from reading, I'll take a good self-help or spirituality book anytime. I guess the common traits I look for in books are that they be educational, inspirational, and/or transformative. Maybe that helps to explain why you'll never see me on an airplane reading the latest bestselling political thriller or celebrity memoir. Call me a literary snob if you will, but it's just not worth my time to read books that don't meet those personally beneficial criteria I outlined.

Proactive Pono

I would submit to you, the reader, that there are two ways of doing the next right thing, one responsive and one proactive. What I mean by that is this: what would be your natural response to someone cutting you off in traffic? Or receiving an overcooked steak in an expensive restaurant? Or being fired from your job? How do you normally answer the telephone or the front door? How do you respond, if at all, to someone if they say, "good morning" to you? How good are you at receiving constructive criticism? These are examples of life situations to which we must choose how we will response. If we can all agree that flipping off a motorist, stiffing a waiter, or telling your boss where he can stick your pink slip, are definitely the wrong way to handle those situations, then it doesn't take much to figure out what the right way might be.

It's very important to remember that we can only control what we put out into the universe - what comes at us oftentimes is completely unexpected and, sometimes, overwhelming. So how do we deal with life on life's terms while trying to stay pono?

Kaiewa

Some years ago, I discovered a Hawaiian word that best sums up my approach to life: *kaiewa*. The *Hawaiian Dictionary* offers this definition of the word: "To take life philosophically as it comes, sometimes in poverty, sometimes in wealth."[8] The philosophy of accepting life on life's terms was one I had learned at an early age. Since neither my parents, nor my teachers, ever suggested to me that life was somehow fair, I grew up with the simple belief that life called all the shots, and that I was just lucky to be allowed to play in her game. One way in which life demonstrated its nonexistent sense of fair play was by instilling within me, throughout my youth, passionate *joie de vivre* - only to throw me a curveball, called cancer, years later. Thanks to my unidentified, yet present, belief in *kaiewa,* I was able to view my life-threatening disease as a mere speed bump, a temporary inconvenience.

Life has no conscience. On Monday, it might allow us to experience the wondrous miracle of the birth of a child, only to take that child away from us (through disease, accident, or war), with no warning or pity, on Tuesday. Without any set of rules to follow or obey, life will see to it that what seems reasonable and right to one person, will simply not be perceived that way by another. Life will masquerade as an intellectual enigma if you let it, or will open its deepest secrets to you just by your willingness to look for and discover its beautiful simplicity.

It is my firm belief that acceptance is the key to living a full life. As a young man I had to learn to accept the fact that the only certainty in life is its uncertainty. I had to accept the fact that life is glorious, cruel, beautiful, evil, fulfilling, and depressing. It possesses all the answers of the universe, yet seems to be reticent in offering them. She comes and goes as she pleases, and her whims are our fate. That is why I resigned myself, years ago, to just be grateful, and content, for whatever time I get to spend with her.

Even with all of life's uncertainties and whims, I will always accept *kaiewa* as the best approach to life, in spite of that game she insists on playing – the one without rules, boundaries, or logic.

Since selfless love is where we began this chapter, I which to end with a prayer about the power of selflessness. It comes from my yoga instructor's Guru:

Sri Swami Satchidananda's Prayer

All I teach is that you learn to be selfless. Your life can be a beautiful fruit for all humanity to enjoy. You can retain the God who is already in you in the form of peace and joy. And when you shine with peace, you expose to that light not only yourself, but other people as well. Let people see something beautiful in you, something genuine in you. Let God be born in you. That's my prayer. Let it begin with you, then let it spread to your community, to your country, and ultimately to the entire globe.[9]

No other words could better describe how *The Pono Principle* works when selflessness is at its core. Amen.

A Pono Life Lesson

This month marks the 50th Anniversary of my starting high school. As a freshman student attending a new school, where I didn't know anyone, it took awhile until I was able to develop friendships with other fellow students. My very small high school was located next to the elementary school where the majority of my classmates and their siblings had attended school together, some since the 1st Grade. Naturally, most of my freshman class had established friendships with each other going back many years, and the few of us who were new to the school were a bit ostracized for that first year or two.

It was not uncommon to witness, and sometimes experience, bullying in such an environment.

By the time I started my junior year I had become friends with several classmates, but that number grew considerably after I started driving. I discovered that having a car was a bit of a fast track to popularity in high school – at least, it was where I went. Once bitten by the popularity bug, it was very easy for me to start distancing myself from the couple of guys I hung around with for those first two years of high school, and start gravitating towards more popular fellow classmates. Sadly, one of the rites of passage common at that time in my high school was to mimic the behavior of some of the perceived "cool" guys who oftentimes picked on several classmates whom they felt superior to. The bullied kid was usually someone who didn't play sports, the straight-A student, the kid who was very effeminate, or someone who was mentally slower than the others.

Although I didn't partake of this behavior with the same fervor shown by some, I have to admit that I did choose to bully several of my classmates just to be more accepted by those "cool" guys. There was one classmate in particular who bore the brunt of the abuse dished out by the bullies in our class. Although I never laid a hand on this person, I do remember getting in trouble one time for shooting him in the eye with a rubber band. I carry the shame of that memory all these many years later.

In writing this chapter on the subject of Doing The Next Right Thing, it occurred to me that I had never made direct amends to this individual whom I had bullied in high school. Even though we both attended our class reunion last year, I neglected to use that opportunity to apologize for my abusive behavior. I truly wish I had. Luckily, after I returned home from the reunion, I was able to find him on social media, and we "friended" each other.

As a recovering alcoholic, I am well aware of the fact that I must make amends to everyone I have ever harmed in my life, even if those things happened almost 50 years ago. I had already made the majority of my Step Nine amends seven years ago, but this particular wrong from my past haunted me still. For me personally, making amends to this particular individual was definitely the *next right thing* that I needed to do. But what does one say to another human being, whom he was guilty of abusing, way back when they were teenage high school students? Would I be opening up old wounds for him? Would my apology appear to be completely self-serving or shallow? Is this a sleeping dog best left undisturbed?

A little over a month ago, I followed my conscience in initiating a pono action step by texting this individual to whom I was responsible for causing pain and suffering. I admitted that I was both guilty and ashamed of my disgusting behavior towards him, and was truly sorry for any memories he might have of me bullying him. Specifically,

I recalled a time when he had phoned me at my parent's house to ask if I wanted to hang out with him, and how I had made up some lame excuse as to why I couldn't. Mind you, this was someone I would sometimes bully at school asking me if we could get together sometime. I can vividly remember that when I hung up the phone, I cried from shame.

I told my classmate that, although I couldn't, I wished I could turn back the hands of time so that I could show him the courtesy that he deserved as a fellow classmate of mine. The best that I could do was to ask for his forgiveness for my disgusting juvenile behavior and to assure him that I am not that type of man today. I also said that I wished I could remove any pain that he felt as a result of my treatment towards him those many years ago. I told him that my prayer was that he could find it in his heart to forgive me, and to know that I will always look forward to seeing him at any future class reunion.

The moment I sent the text to my classmate, I knew that I had just done something very special, very right. By the grace of God, my classmate responded to my text, thanking me for sending it, but also letting me know that all of these things happened a long time ago, and he had forgotten most of it. I told him that I was glad for that, and I thanked him for his response. You see, sometimes the *next* right thing isn't what happens right after the *last* right thing you just finished doing. Sometimes it takes several days to get around to it. And sometimes it might take 50 years. The bottom line is that it's *still* the right thing to do – so why put it off another minute?

True Self-Realization

Chapter 3

Who Am I, Really?

Where is the man who will do the right
thing, no matter what the cost?
- Charles Marshall

So, in a nutshell – what we learn in life we learn by observing the world around us. We then think about what we have learned and, hopefully, find a lesson in the learning. Ideally, that life lesson will inspire us to consciously act in a manner that benefits ourselves, others, and the world we share together – something I call *The Pono Principle.* Now, the big question is: Who is this *act*-or, this *do*-gooder, this person dedicated to doing the next right thing?

I can tell you who that person isn't. He isn't the false self that I was for the majority of my life - the selfish, self-centered, self-absorbed individual who always thought of himself before anyone - and everyone - else. That guy didn't care about anyone, except himself. Oh, he *absolutely* loved his wife, his children, and his friends. The problem was that he *absolutely* put *his* wants and desires before any of theirs. As a man suffering from addiction, he possessed all of the character defects shared by addicts - selfishness and self-centeredness being at the core. You see, addicts wrote the book on how to portray their false selves to the rest of the world. They are like professional Shakespearian actors, caught in a theatrical Twilight Zone, doomed to perpetually portray only the most tragic of characters. That is, until the final curtain – when they either die from their addictions, or they willingly take off their masks and costumes, and unveil their true selves behind the masks.

The false actor I was for most of my life made his final curtain call in 2010, the year when I accepted the truth of my addictions, and finally *did* something about them. Since then, I have been on a spiritual quest – a journey to find my true self, the man God created me to be. Through diligent recovery work, and the love and support of countless friends and family, I have dedicated myself to discovering who I *really* am. By first deconstructing my false self, I was only then prepared to rebuild on the foundation of my true self. I will share with you the road that I have taken - the one to finding my true self - by reflecting back over 40 years ago, when I first started college, and learned my first truth.

I Am, the First Truth

In the early days of my college education, I fell in love with Philosophy. What I most remember about those first introductory Philosophy courses was that one could logically question just about anything: the existence of God, the existence of others, or whether an object could ever get from Point A to Point B (when there were an infinite number of points between A and B for the object to traverse). But the one thing, the one truth, that I discovered could not be logically questioned, was one's own existence. René Descartes, the French philosopher, was responsible for that first, and most profound, truth I learned in college: *Cogito ergo sum (I think, therefore I am.).* In sum, Descartes reasoned that the fact that I can question my own existence proves that I exist. Each and every Philosophy professor I had during college agreed that this was a truth that I could hang my hat on.

As I grew older, and began to read Scripture, I realized that the one indisputable Truth that I learned in college, the self-identifying "I am," echoed throughout the Bible like a clarion bell. When Moses asks God by what name he should call Him, God replies, "I AM WHO I AM. This is what you are to say to the Israelites:

'I AM has sent me to you'"[10] (Exodus 3:14 NIV). Naturally, it was no surprise to find that the Incarnation of God, Jesus Christ, used the exact same self-descriptive when He told the Jews in the temple, "Very truly I tell you, before Abraham was born, I am!"[11] (John 8:58 NIV).

Like Father, like Son - like me.

"Here I am *(Hineni)*," the Pono Response

One of the most powerful Hebrew words found in the Bible is *Hineni* (הנני), which means "Here I am!" As used throughout the Old Testament, it is a way of expressing total readiness to give oneself to God's calling – it's an offer of complete availability to God. When God called out to Abraham, Jacob, Moses, Samuel, and Isaiah, they all responded with the exact same word, *Hineni* ("Here I am"). Most Biblical scholars would probably suggest that "Here I am" is a very receptive reply to a summons from the Almighty. The tone of the response seems to suggest, "Yes, Lord, how may I be of service to You?"

Perhaps this is a silly point, but I'm going to make it anyway: My writer's inclination is to want to place a comma after the word *Here* (as in "Here, I AM") so as to change the direction, and the focus, of the response from me back to God. The comma allows me to change who the "I am" is in the reply. When I was in the Army, we had morning formations, where the First Sergeant would do roll call. When he would call a soldier's last name, you were expected to bark out your reply, "Here, First Sergeant!" That emphatic response was exactly what was expected, and demanded, of every soldier in morning formation. So, when I imagine these Biblical heroes of the Old Testament being summoned by God, and immediately answering to His gentle whisper, I can't help but view them as being nothing less than the best, most responsive Soldiers for God – with or without a comma in their reply.

A Few Shakespearean Pono Precepts

In Act 1, Scene 3 of William Shakespeare's *Hamlet,* Polonius is saying farewell to his son, Laertes, who is bound for France. He gives Laertes his blessing, and then offers a "few precepts" concerning "character." Polonius's advice reads like a juxtaposition of common sense principles: keep your thoughts to yourself, but don't act on your stupid ones; be openly friendly with others, but don't be vulgar; keep your true friends close to you, but don't waste your time on false ones; try not to get into fights, but, if you do, win them; always listen to others, but speak only when necessary; accept criticism from others, but don't judge them in kind; look your best, but don't spend lots of money on fancy clothing; don't borrow money from others, and don't lend it to them either. Here, Polonius saves the best advice for last, "This above all – to thine own self be true, And it must follow, as the night the day, Thou canst not then be false to any man."[12]

With that closing line of fatherly advice, Polonius emphasizes how important it is that Laertes stick to his principles, and that he always does what he knows is right. It's the old peer pressure speech we all got from our parents, especially when we went off to college. "Just because your roommate offers you arsenic, doesn't mean you have to drink it" was something my parents would have said in those early years of the 70s. I can't believe how relieved my parents were when, after coming home from college, I was able to report that I never once succumbed to the strong temptation to drink arsenic. Thank God they never asked about all the *other* drugs and alcohol I so willingly partook of during those years.

Our Many Selves

The "self" that Polonius was referring to, in *Hamlet,* the one that he advises Laertes to be true to, was singular in nature. I am fairly confident that when Shakespeare wrote this play, he thought of the *self* as a singular concept. But in today's world of personal transformation, addiction recovery, and spiritual enlightenment, we have come to view the *self* as a binary entity, one that starts in one dimension and, potentially, evolves into a more desirable one. Different writers, and different spiritual philosophies, will use different terms for the "binary selves" to illustrate their beliefs:

- False Self / True Self (Artificial Self / Real Self)
- Human Self / Divine Self (Ego Self / God Self)
- Lower Self / Higher Self
- Personal Self / Impersonal Self
- Corrupted Self / Pure Self
- Finite Self / Infinite Self
- Old Self / New Self

Years ago, people would have referred to this notion of *self* as some form of having split personalities, but in modern usage these terms are used to identify the *self* we used to be, and the one we hope to become someday.

Transforming From the Ego-Self to the God-Self

Wise people have always passed through a major death to their egocentricity. This is the core meaning of transformation.
— Richard Rohr

Some say, "The *ego* is the distance we put between ourselves and God." Others will say, "*Sin* is the distance we put between ourselves and God." Since God is completely blameless for our selfish, ego-driven sins, I would suggest that both of those statements are patently true. In short, the Ego-Self is always the problem, and the God-Self is always the answer. They are on opposite ends of the transformation spectrum, and only by surrendering the one (the Ego-Self) will we

ever be able to find a victorious spiritual transformation towards the
other (the God-Self). This is the common bond shared by almost
every spiritual religion and recovery program in the world. Not until
we model the lives of the saints and sages (all of whom followed this
spiritual pathway) - by destroying our Ego-Selves and focusing our
lives on service to others - will we discover God residing in our souls.
That is where He has always resided, just waiting for us to "Love
each other as I have loved you"[13] (John 15:12 NIV).

It's All About Service

One time, Sri Swami Satchidananda was asked, "What is the best
way to serve God while living in the world?" The revered Guru replied,

> *Serve one and all. Then you will have served God.*
> *Don't even lose a single opportunity to serve others.*
> *Serve, serve, serve, and you will find that you also are*
> *served.*[14]

Stop right now and imagine a list of people who might have
answered this question with the exact same response – Jesus, the
Dalai Lama, Gandhi, Bill Wilson, Mother Teresa, your parish priest
or minister, and every saint and sage throughout history. Would you
consider these people to be spiritual role models, individuals whose
advice you might wish to take to heart? I certainly hope so.

The last portion of the quote from Swami Satchidananda has to
do with the personal reward experienced by those who serve others.
I can tell you from my own history, prior to recovery, that service to
others was only of interest *to* me when there was a financial benefit
for me. As a waiter of many years, I certainly qualified to be able
to say that I was in the *service* business, albeit for wages and tips.
That's a far cry from saying that I do volunteer *service* by feeding the
homeless and homebound (which I do now). In other words, my past

Ego-Self was a paid waiter, whereas my present-day God-Self is still serving food to people, but without any financial reimbursement. The difference between my personal *reward* for feeding others in an upscale restaurant, versus my spiritual *reward* for feeding others in need, is immeasurable. To have a homeless man or woman look you in the eye and say, "Thank you for what you do" is to hear the voice of an angel, a reward beyond worldly riches.

Now, here's the rub. The moment I start seeking those *thank yous*, or feel slighted when I don't get them, I'm in trouble. There's a huge difference between feeling appreciated for services rendered versus feeling unappreciated for the same acts – the former is a bonus which can be humbly accepted, while the latter should never to be expected, and certainly shouldn't be a motivator for doing good works. In the words of Swami Satchidananda, "Service is just one-sided. You just give for the sake of giving; no expectation whatsoever."[15] Whether I receive *thank yous* (or not) from the homebound whom I delivery food to every week, I always thank God for giving me the opportunity just to serve – and that's good enough for me.

Sacred Illnesses

Illness is a story. It calls us to healing beyond our physical selves. A strange contradiction. Suffering from an affliction invites us to step into a realm of healing that can benefit ourselves, our community and the world. Illness is, therefore, at the very core of healing. Not a contradiction but the strange dance of creation.

With these words, Deena Metzger opened her keynote address at the annual convocation of the American Academy of Osteopathy, in Birmingham, Alabama, in March of 2006. Twenty-nine years earlier, at the age of 40, Deena was diagnosed with breast cancer.

Rather than putting her body through the ravages of chemotherapy or radiation, Deena chose to have a mastectomy. How her cancer (her illness) helped her to heal herself, and the community of others whom she has taught and counseled for over four decades, defines her life's work. What Deena discovered was that her life-threatening cancer experience forced her to scrutinize her life, heart and soul, and consequently deepened her sense of joy, purpose, and meaning. She so firmly believes that her cancer experience actually enhanced and extended her life, that she refers to her illness as being *sacred:*

> *A sacred illness is one that educates and alters us from the inside out, provides experiences and therefore knowledge that we could not possibly achieve in any other way, and aligns us with a life path that is, ultimately, of benefit to ourselves and those around us.*

Over the course of my lifetime, I have been blessed with two sacred illnesses, cancer and alcoholism. One illness (cancer) took me 42 years to get, the other (alcoholism) 41 years to get rid of. I have known the life-transforming healing benefits of cancer for well over 20 years now, and the healing powers found in alcohol recovery for over seven years (as of this writing). Without question, I am a much better man for having had these two sacred illnesses.

Prior to my cancer experience, I was a very self-centered individual who was emotionally indifferent to the plight of others. When tragedy befell other people, the best emotional response I was able to muster, in those days, was something along the line of, "Too bad for them." It wasn't until I myself, at the age of 42, was diagnosed with Stage 4-B Hodgkin's Disease (mind you, there is no "5" or "C" in cancer staging) that I developed a sense of compassion for others that had, until then, escaped me. I started to appreciate the work of doctors more, the "angels on earth" commonly referred to as nurses, and, mostly, I started to care about those other cancer patients who were fighting for their lives like I was. What an amazing gift from

God that was. Perhaps the greatest *gift* of my cancer scare was that it was the first time in my life that I had to face my own mortality, and *accept* the possibility that I might die at the age of 42.

During those six months of chemotherapy injections in my oncologist's office, I was very cognizant of the fact that several of the other cancer patients that were also receiving treatment there, did not survive - while I did. Perhaps the harshest reality was that several of my fellow patients were much younger than I. Even though I was never one to give credence to the *fairness* argument as to why some people die from deadly diseases and accidents, while others survive, what I did discover about myself was that I was developing internal feelings of empathy and compassion towards my fellow cancer patients. This was quite a revelation to one as self-centered as I at that time of my life.

My personal healing from the sacred illness of cancer began with my desire to become active in a cancer support group at my local hospital – my first pono action step. That evolved into a desire to fund-raise for the Leukemia and Lymphoma Society's Team-in-Training program, which further evolved into my being on that organization's Board of Trustees for six years – more pono action steps. Cancer taught me how to savor moments with my family at a whole new level, how to express gratitude more openly, and accept the fact that every day I was given, after my cancer went into remission, was an additional gift from God. Today, as I look back upon my cancer scare, I see it for what it truly was – merely a temporary inconvenience. For whatever His reason, God willed me to have the disease, to fight through it, and to survive it. If the reason was so that I might learn something of humility, then I will be the first to say that it was worth the experience, for I believe the gift of humility may be the most necessary virtue for spiritual transformation.

Likewise, when I was a self-centered alcoholic, I didn't care much about the problems of my drinking buddies, and certainly didn't care about how alcohol ruined the lives of faceless other people around the globe. "Too bad for them." When I was finally willing to admit that *I* was powerless over alcohol, that *I* suffered from the disease of alcoholism, it was only then that *I* started to show compassion towards other alcoholics. Suddenly, strangers who had been in and out of alcohol and drug rehab centers were of concern to me, ex-cons made up my after-meeting coffee klatch, and people who had been beaten into the dirt by alcohol were my newfound friends. Another gift from God.

My personal healing from the sacred illness of alcoholism began with my desire to become active in an addiction recovery program. By volunteering to serve many times as secretary of group sessions, speaking at meetings whenever invited to do so, helping to clean up after meetings, and by sponsoring other alcoholics, I have found healing from my illness through service to others.

The bonus blessing in all of this is that I'm not the only one who has benefited from my healing experience. Sure, I've become a more compassionate human being as a result of my two sacred illnesses, and that has helped me to be a fuller, more caring man. But the ripples from whatever newfound compassion I have demonstrated over these past years, simply through cause and effect, have spread from my actions to the benefit of those around me. In other words, the gift of healing that I have received has been passed on to others.

At this time, I wish to reiterate what I have often said about my two sacred illnesses: I am so very grateful to God for having had cancer, and for being an alcoholic. Without those two blessings in my life, I would never have learned humility nor compassion. Like Deena Metzger, if I had never had my sacred illnesses, I could never have possibly achieved the knowledge, nor the healing, that those illnesses freely gave me. Only by my having suffered through those afflictions, have I been invited "to step into a realm of healing that can benefit ourselves, our community and the world."

So, what have I learned so far?

I AM. I AM HERE. I AM HERE TO SERVE OTHERS.

A Pono Life Lesson

Perhaps the most famous image of God and Man, together but still separated, is *The Creation of Adam*, the fresco painting that adorns the ceiling of the Sistine Chapel in Rome. Michelangelo says so much about the relationship between God and Man by depicting their contrasting concave/convex postures, their near-touching hands, and the difference in their perceived demeanor. Whereas God is shown strenuously reaching out towards His creation, Adam's down-turned bent fingers denote an almost arrogant indifference towards his Creator. God appears to be the only one interested in bridging the space between them, wanting desperately to connect and be one with Man - while Adam looks like he's merely worn out from his 90-minute massage at the health spa.

For most of my life, I had the same kind of *limp wrist* towards God that Adam has in the painting. Whatever distance I perceived as existing between me and God, I created myself. I have never doubted for one moment that God has never stopped reaching out to me my entire lifetime. It was solely *my* ego, and *my* sins, that pushed Him away from my self-centered consciousness. Whenever I have felt separated from God, it was because I had no God Consciousness, which is the opposite of Ego Consciousness, the very thing that ruled my life for many years.

So what has changed in my life? When did I finally allow God back into my life? How did the discovery of my first truth (that "I am") eventually lead me to the discovery of the ultimate truth (that I am *one* with the Great "I AM")? At what point in my life did I hear God's whisper and respond, "Here I am?" In other words, when did I finally extend my fingers and reach out to the hand of God – the hand that has eternally been extended to me?

Many organized religions find it necessary to perpetuate the dogmatic belief that the nature of God and Man are two separate entities. This very limited construct represents God as nothing more than an eternal omnipotent being who demands exclusive adulation from His creation, while Man is relegated to being only a sinful mortal who must obey the commands of his Creator, or face eternal damnation. At least, that pretty well sums up the God that I was taught to worship in my own religion. That is certainly not the image I have of God today.

After many years of studying spirituality, yoga, and other organized religions, I have come to believe that true self-realization comes only when an individual finally *realizes* that "the Self is God."[16] To further quote Sri Swami Satchidananda, "You realize that the soul and God are one and the same." Instead of limiting our understanding to there being only two natures – that of God and Man – one comes to realize that there is a *third party,* a *common nature,* that according to Emerson, "is God:"

> *Ineffable is the union of man and God in every act of the soul. The simplest person, who in his integrity worships God, becomes God.*[17]

No doubt that this belief flies in the face of what many religious and spiritual people believe - not to mention every atheist and, probably, most agnostics - but I can only share how God has presented Himself to me personally. Mind you, my God Consciousness (or Divine Consciousness) was completely blocked by 57 years of obsessive Ego Consciousness. Basically, what had to happen was for my False Self to die completely before my True Self could come to light. All those wasted years that I spent seeking peace, joy, and love somewhere *outside* myself - and the whole time those desired qualities rested *within* my soul, where I found God residing.

Where else would the Great I AM choose to be? How many artisans, craftsmen, and inventors, have said that there's always a part of them that lives inside each and every one of their handcrafted creations? They all say that. Why do you think that the voice of God comes to us as a gentle whisper? Think about how close you really have to be to someone for him or her to hear your gentle whisper. You don't get any closer than when you reside inside one's soul.

Who am I, really? I am merely the instrument of my Creator's will, the one who keeps his ears open so as to discover His will, and then to act on it. And what exactly is God's will? Just this:

GO AND DO THE NEXT RIGHT THING

Recovery

Unity

Service

A Fellowship of Pono

Chapter 4

Pono In Recovery

When I am willing to do the right thing, I am rewarded with
an inner peace no amount of liquor could ever provide.
- Alcoholics Anonymous, p. 317

As a recovering alcoholic I can honestly state that I owe much of my sobriety success to a much-repeated maxim that alcoholics in recovery are constantly reminded of – just do the next right thing. Certainly, repeating the wrong things we did during our drinking years is not an option for those who wish to change their lives for the better. After all, as we hear time and again, it was our *best* thinking that got us here in the first place. Therefore, practicing pono in our new sober way of thinking is a must.

What many find in addiction recovery is that the answer to sobriety had been staring them in the face their entire lives – simply knowing right from wrong. It would be nearly impossible to imagine addicts who didn't know that it was wrong for them to lie to their spouses as to where they were all night. That it was wrong to drink and drive. That it was wrong to steal money from their mothers' purses in order to buy drugs, or to steal medication from their parents' medicine cabinets. These were some of the common sins of addicts who, now in recovery, choose to make amends for by not ever repeating them. More importantly, recovering addicts realize that they must live pono from now on.

Doing the next right thing in recovery mirrors what I have always known to be the correct way to live. I am reminded that I have always known the right way to go in life but, during my years of addiction, my stinking thinking took me down side trails that proved disastrous for me and those closest to me. Only now, possessing a clear sober mind, do I realize that *The Pono Principle* is what guides me along that right way to the life I was meant to live.

On June 21, 2010, I made what has proven to be one of the most important decisions of my life. For 41 years, I had abused alcohol and drugs while, simultaneously, trying to play the role of a responsible loving husband, father, friend, employee, and business owner. The simple truth that I had to accept on that June day was the fact that I was powerless over alcohol and that my life had become unmanageable. Due to addiction, my defects of character and personal shortcomings had prevented me from being the man that God had created me to be. But because I have stayed committed to a program of recovery ever since that date, I can honestly say that *The Pono Principle* has been the primary key to my progress.

At the heart of my recovery program is the constant reminder to do the next right thing or, as Hawaiians would say, be pono. Whatever one's addiction of choice, the one guiding principle that has been demonstrated to effectively transform destructive behavior to a life of purpose is the shift from merely making plans (while worrying about the outcome), to focusing on doing the next right thing (and trusting that the outcome will take care of itself). That's a huge part of The 12-Step Program's Step Three – "Made a decision to turn our will and our lives over to the care of God as we understood Him."[18] When trying to determine what is the right thing to do, some addicts let their conscience be their guide, while others might rely on The Golden Rule, or pray for guidance to be shown the right thing.

What I have discovered is that, when I am focused on doing the right thing, I have far more peace of mind, and a far greater chance of staying sober. That's because I have seen the rewards of being and living pono. The mere fact that I chose to do the right thing by giving up my addictions has, in itself, changed my life in a miraculous way. To then be able to acknowledge the destructive behavior I had been responsible for, during my drinking career, was yet another necessary right thing to do. The reward for that action has been an honest self-awareness I had never known before sobriety. Ultimately, the greatest act of pono, in my recovery, has been my unconditional surrender of ego in exchange for God's will for me. First, I'll address my definition of ego, and then I'll talk about when I finally turned my life over to God's will.

Ego (Edging God Out)

It's been said that ego is the distance we put between God and ourselves. I believe that to be true. I know what it is to be a selfish, prideful man. I know what it is to think only of myself. As shameful as my admission is, it does truthfully describe the alcoholic I was for most of my life. Therefore, within that confession I am also admitting that, because of my over-inflated ego, my relationship with God was not a close one. I was solely responsible for distancing myself from God, not vice versa.

When I finally sought recovery in 2010, the first word I learned in the program was *We.* I guess some would say there is no "I" in recovery (maybe the spelling of the word should be changed to *we*-covery). Even though I spent 41 years with an obsession of self (ego), *I* was never able to find the road to recovery by my *self;* only God, and other fellow alcoholics, were able to show me the way. This realization was a shattering ego deflator, and the best thing that ever happened to me. Almost immediately, I felt a closeness to God that I had never known before.

By no means am I suggesting that my ego has been put in check. What I am saying is that my reliance upon God's will in my life (which produces positive results), versus my reliance upon self-will (which has produced most of the problems in my life), is directly proportional to the amount of ego I display at any given time. Ego may be the best example of where less is more.

Some years ago, I initiated a new way to start and end each day. The very first thing I do in the morning is to get on my knees, and say *Please* to God ("Please, God, give me the strength to stay sober today. Please give me the compassion to help anyone less fortunate than I."). At the end of the day, again on my knees, I say *Thank you* to God ("Thank you, God, for your countless blessings. Thank you for another day of sobriety.") The last words I say at the end of both my morning and evening prayers are, "May Thy will, not mine, be done. Amen."

Few things in this world humble a man more than getting on his knees before God, in either an act of supplication or an act of gratitude. Only by lowering my *self* before God, by getting on my knees, is my ego lifted away, and the distance between me and God reduced to what can be heard in the whisper of a prayer.

God is My Chauffeur

One of the great World War Two autobiographies, *God is My Co-Pilot,* was written by Colonel Robert L. Scott, Jr. in 1943. The story is about Colonel Scott's war experience as an ace pilot with the Flying Tigers in China and Burma. I only mention the book because its title so adequately describes my view of God throughout most of my life.

Before sobriety, I thought of myself as the pilot of my own life, solely in control of the course, and direction, I was going to steer it. My view of God was that of my co-pilot, a source of help sitting next to me, should I need to turn to Him in emergency situations. It would never have occurred to me then, that He might have a better road map for my life than I. After all, He was *only* the co-pilot.

My view of God changed course dramatically during the early days of my recovery. After accepting my powerlessness over alcohol, I also had to accept that I (the pilot) was solely responsible for my life being unmanageable. In other words, my ignoring all of the signs that I was off-course for most of my life's *flight,* and coming dangerously close to crashing several times, led me to accept that I needed to turn to God (my co-pilot). This was the emergency situation where I finally turned to Him for help. And all the while, there He was sitting next to me, patiently waiting.

After sobriety, I tendered my pilot wings to God and surrendered my desire to fly the wild blue yonder any longer. For whatever amount of time I have remaining in this life, I will travel my life's course closer to the ground, in a car. But I won't be driving that car. I have learned through recovery that I am no more qualified to drive a car than I was to pilot an airplane. When I made the decision to turn my will and my life over to the care of God, it was like I had tossed the car keys to God and said, "Here, you drive."

God is now my chauffeur. Every morning He greets me with a smile, opens the rear car door for me, I get inside, He gets in the driver's seat, and then He asks me where I would like to go. As tempting as it is to immediately start thinking of places that tickle my fancy, I find myself these days looking at His eyes in the rear-view mirror and saying, "Wherever you'd like to take me. After all, you know the road much better than I."

The Sin of a Self-Centered Son

On September 2, 1974, I was in Toronto, at Varsity Stadium, listening to Jesse Colin Young, The Band, and Crosby, Stills, Nash, and Young, in the cold rain. Where I should have been was back home, in St. Clair Shores, Michigan, putting together the final touches for a party I was supposed to throw for my parents' 25th Wedding Anniversary - which was the next day. I'm embarrassed to admit that, to this day, I have absolutely no idea what my parents did for that very special anniversary. All I know is, I wasn't there because it was more important to me to be at the Labour Day Show, at Varsity Stadium, and pay $12.00 to stand in the rain.

In September 1974, I was 21 years old and one year out of the Army. My best friend from the Army, Terry, had just been discharged, and he and I took the train from Windsor to Toronto to go to the concert. It is not an exaggeration that CSN&Y was my favorite rock group in those days, and the main reason I taught myself how to play acoustic guitar while I was in the Army.

That said, what kind of a son leaves the responsibility of throwing his parents a 25th Wedding Anniversary party to his 12-year-old brother? That is exactly what I did when I hopped on that train with Terry, bound for Toronto. In other words, *I* was that kind of a son. How could I possibly do that to my parents, the two people who had sacrificed so much over the past 21 years, to see to it that my brother and I never wanted for anything? I'll tell you.

Like many 21-year-olds, whether of that era or later, I was unapologetically egocentric. Truth be told, I was still pretty egocentric for another 36 years after that sad affair. Now, just in case *egocentric* is too Freudian a term for some, let's call it what is was – selfishness and self-centeredness. And here lies the saddest truth of all. Until I became sober, if I would have been accused of being a selfish and self-centered individual, I would have arrogantly responded, "Yeah, so what?" Until I finally addressed my alcoholic character defects, I didn't see the sin of being so self-centered. Not until I read page 62 of Bill Wilson's life-changing *Alcoholics Anonymous* (1939), did the light bulb finally go on in my head: "Selfishness – self-centeredness! That, we think, is the root of our troubles."[19]

For this recovering alcoholic, those 11 words may have been the clearest revelation of truth that I had ever experienced. They were certainly responsible for my accepting the fact that I was powerless over alcohol and that my life had become unmanageable. What those 11 words validated for me is that I belonged in that fellowship of other recovering addicts who also used to be selfish, self-centered individuals. What a gift those words were to me.

Of course, there is absolutely nothing that I can do today to undo the hurt my parents must have felt over forty years ago, as a direct result of my selfish, self-centered behavior. I was still an alcoholic when my parents died in 1999 and 2000. Even if I had apologized to them, which I probably did at some point in time, it could never fix the broken plate of my mother and fathers' hearts.

My mother was the type of women who believed, as Jenny Cavalleri did in *Love Story,* that "Love means never having to say you're sorry." She would have excused my selfish behavior, and accepted my meaningless apology, simply because I was her beloved son. God knows, she probably overlooked the vast majority of my character defects for that reason alone.

In addiction recovery, we realize that, during our drinking careers, all of our apologies (no matter how sincere) were worthless; our families and friends will be the first to attest to that. That is why we make direct amends to all those we have harmed. Amends are about a genuine change in our behavior instead of the patchwork of an apology. And when direct amends are not possible, as in my case, we make living amends. That simply means that we live differently, that we amend the way we live the rest of our lives. We choose to live a whole new way of life, a life of honesty and integrity, where apologies are replaced by amends, and amends are seldom necessary. In other words, we choose to live pono.

Character – From Being One to Finding It

The etymology of the word *character* comes from the Greek *kharaktēr,* a stamping tool used to make a distinctive mark or impression on something. *Character* is always used as a noun, but has the distinction of both defining a certain type of person, while also representing an admirable quality that distinguishes one person from another. As to the former usage of the word, a character most often defines a person in a novel, play, or film - although, more informally, it also describes an eccentric or amusing person (as in "Boy, that guy's a real character"). As a stage actor, and an alcoholic, this was the type of *character* that most often applied to me during my drinking career. It is well worth noting that, during those same years, the latter use of the word was seldom, if ever, used to describe my personal "qualities." In his "Big Book," *Alcoholics Anonymous* (1939), Bill Wilson states,

> *More than most people, the alcoholic leads a double life. He is very much the actor. To the outer world he presents his stage character. This is the one he likes his fellows to see. He wants to enjoy a certain reputation, but knows in his heart he doesn't deserve it.*[20]

With this statement, Bill Wilson is discussing Step Five of The 12-Step Program ("Admitted to God, to ourselves, and to another human being the exact nature of our wrongs"[21]). How true that description fit me during my years of drinking. The actor in me desired to portray myself to the outside world as a fun-loving *bon vivant*, one who could embellish stories like a novelist, wax poetic on any subject, and captivate the world with my intellect and charm. Of course, in my self-serving portrayal of this *character*, there was little need for such selfless qualities like honesty or humility. What use has a *real* character of those virtues?

And so, precisely because of my selfish, self-serving, self-promoting, self-centeredness (redundancy intended and appropriate), the character that I played, as masterful as Olivier could have, was unfortunately as tragic as his Hamlet. The sad irony in the stage play of my 41-year alcoholic *run* was that the selfish character that I played was unable to display selfless character. In other words, although alcohol had been responsible in creating my bigger-than-life character, it had contributed nothing in building *true* character within me as a man. That virtuous quality was never fully accessible to me because of my disease and, thus, I was a stranger to my own true self.

In a letter to his wife Alice, William James wrote in 1878,

*I have often thought that the best way to define a man's
character would be to seek out the particular mental or
moral attitude in which, when it came upon him, he
felt himself most deeply and intensely active and alive.
At such moments there is a voice inside which speaks
and says: 'This is the real me!'[22]*

Now is such a moment for me. At this stage of my sobriety, I
can truthfully say that I have never been more "deeply and intensely
active and alive." I have no reservations stating that I am more
honestly self-aware today than at any other time in my life and
that, for the first time, I am willing to fully acknowledge both
my good *and* bad qualities. In recovery parlance, we call our bad
qualities *character defects*. In order for the recovering alcoholic to
truly become the person God created him to be, he must commit
himself entirely to character-building by not only asking God for the
strength to do the constructive work he needs to do on himself, but
by also asking God to remove those things that stand in his way to
self-realization – his defects of character. Step Seven addresses this,
and is summed up in a prayer:

*My Creator, I am now willing that you should have
all of me, good and bad. I pray that you now remove
from me every single defect of character which stands
in the way of my usefulness to you and my fellows.
Grant me strength, as I go out from here, to do your
bidding. Amen.[23]*

Ultimately though, it is the individual who must uncover, and
discover, his true self and his true character. In a July 15, 1944, entry
in her *Diary,* Anne Frank rightly observed, "Parents can only give
good advice or put them on the right paths, but the final forming
of a person's character lies in their own hands."[24]

Today, I am very grateful for no longer being thought of in terms of *being* a character like I was during my drinking years. Instead, I now have the ability to practice *having* character in everything I do by staying sober, living a principled life, and doing the next right thing. These action steps, which help form whatever character I may possess, do indeed lie in my "own hands," and truly do define "the real me."

A Pono Life Lesson

As I stated earlier, my sobriety date is June 21, 2010. By the grace of God, I have not had a drop of alcohol since that date. That said, being new to recovery back then, I thought it might still be okay to smoke a little weed to compensate for the huge *sacrifice* I was making by giving up my liquid high. I mean, seriously, wasn't I still allowed to hold on to some form of substance high to get me by? (I'm grinning as I'm writing this). Certainly no one expected me to spend the rest of my life *completely* sober, right? I soon discovered that it doesn't work that way in addiction recovery.

During my first thirty days of recovery, I was quite resistant to the idea that I belonged in an addiction program. I had a very hard time accepting the fact that I might be the type of person who couldn't control his drinking and drug use. I had also never considered the possibility that I might have had not one, but several, addictions that needed to be addressed and combatted.

The way that I discovered my others addictions, during those first thirty days after putting a plug in the jug, was when I noticed how much more pot I was smoking (to substitute for the high I was no longer getting from alcohol), and in how much sugary food I was eating. Of course, it doesn't take a rocket scientist to figure out that the increased amount of pot that I was smoking only led to an increased volume of munchies that I was craving. The simple math of addiction was clear – by giving up one addiction, I had only caved in to, and accelerated, two others (i.e. drugs and food). Not a good way to start an addiction recovery program.

During those first thirty days, a potential sponsor told me that he would only consider sponsoring me if I went to ninety recovery meetings in ninety days. Because of my resistance to doing any kind of recovery work, for a disease I wasn't convinced I even had, I pretty much laughed off the idea of going to *so* many meetings. Certainly, the last thing I wanted to do was to obsess over this whole alcohol issue ("I guess I'll just smoke another doobie so that I don't have to think about this *other* addiction that I *may* suffer from"). Complete insanity.

The questions that I was resistant to ask myself were: At what point am I willing to accept that I suffer from addiction(s), and that my life has suffered as a result? How willing am I to take action steps to combat my addiction(s)? Am I just *done* with my addiction(s), or am I truly *done done?* Am I merely substituting one addiction for another? How willing am I to seriously be *done done* with *all* of my addictions, and to do whatever it takes to transform myself into the individual God created me to be?

As stated, my first thirty days of sobriety were riddled with resistance and self-denial. I may have stopped drinking, but I had merely substituted pot as a means to get high. I hadn't completely surrendered to the fact that I was powerless over alcohol, nor was I willing to do the work asked of me to go to ninety recovery meetings in ninety days. I was your typical dry drunk, someone who thinks that just not drinking is good enough. In addiction recovery parlance, "DRY" is an acronym for "Doing Recovery Yourself" – it seldom, if ever, works for the alcoholic. But something *did* work, and it happened thirty days into my recovery.

Since I was 18 years old, I have been a huge Ernest Hemingway fan. I studied Hemingway in college, have read most everything he has written, and even named my California restaurant after him. Naturally, my family knows this about me. They also know that I have celebrated Hemingway's birthday (July 21st) several times in Paris, using his memoir *A Moveable Feast* as my travel guide. Thirty days into my sobriety was Hemingway's birthday, and I received a text from my middle daughter.

During that summer, my daughter had been working as a volunteer in Tanzania, teaching in a school for mentally challenged children. Before she left for Africa, I gave her a copy of Hemingway's *Green Hills of Africa* and *Snows of Kilimanjaro*. On July 21st, she texted me to say that, without any training whatsoever, she had successfully summited Mount Kilimanjaro - on Hemingway's birthday. I remember that text as though it was yesterday, and I remember crying when I received it.

Immediately, I drove to a recovery meeting, called my prospective sponsor and told him that I was going to the first of my ninety meetings in ninety days. After all, if my daughter could summit the highest mountain on the African continent, without any training, how could I not make every effort to summit the formidable mountain that I needed to climb? After that meeting, I drove home and flushed the last of my pot down the toilet. I firmly committed to working my recovery program and I have never looked back since. In many ways, the truth I learned that day inspired me to continuously work at the most pono thing I can do for my family – to stay clean and sober for the rest of my life.

Owner Serves

Employee
Serves

Customer is
Served

True Customer Service

Chapter 5

Pono In The Workplace

Character is doing the right thing when nobody's looking. There are too many people who think that the only thing that's right is to get by, and the only thing that's wrong is to get caught.

- J. C. Watts

I spent thirteen years in the restaurant profession, four of those as the sole proprietor of a charming, award-winning European café in Northern California. Having been a waiter in many well-to-do restaurants on the Monterey Peninsula, I was trained by some of the most professional and respected owners and dining room managers in the business. One of the first things that I was taught was that there was a right way to set a table, and a wrong way. There was a right way to open a bottle of wine, and a wrong way. You get the idea.

Naturally, this right way/wrong way teaching method was most strictly adhered to in the best restaurants I worked at. Believe me, in some posh eateries it was not uncommon to be fired from your job if it was your third warning that you weren't keeping the salt and pepper shakers on your tables completely filled at all times. In those types of establishments, job security was entirely based on how focused a waiter was on doing things the right way, and at all times.

In these examples, pono is used more in the sense of the proper way of doing something, in perfect order, without any moral or virtuous considerations. Even though it would be correct to say that there is a pono way of setting a table properly, by no means does that infer that society somehow will morally benefit because the knife and spoon are set to the right of the dinner plate, and not to the left.

Nor will the world come to an abrupt end simply because the last residue of lipstick wasn't completely wiped clean from a wineglass. But don't try to sell that to the French sommelier who spots the egregious oversight.

Once I transitioned from being a waiter to owning my own restaurant, my sense of doing what was right also took on a nobler transformation. Although I was still a disciple of classic European table service, and trained my staff accordingly, I was now far more focused on doing right by the customer. How welcome do I make my customers feel when they first walk through the front door of my establishment? How friendly is my staff towards them at their table? How attentive are they to the customers' needs?

There's an old axiom in the restaurant business that "the customer is always right, even when they're wrong." Believe me, there is nothing more frustrating for a restaurant owner, waiter, or chef to deal with than a customer who sends a pink-centered steak back to the kitchen because it's "overcooked," and not "Medium" liked she ordered. Of course, the tactful way of dealing with this classic restaurant occurrence is for the owner or waiter (definitely NOT the chef), to calmly explain to the customer that if she wanted a juicier, more reddish center to her steak, she should have ordered it Medium-Rare, not Medium. This would be the preferred *right* way of dealing with this situation. Having the chef involved in the conversation would be an historical disaster.

Here is where practicing pono in the workplace takes on a more humane character. Few things make me feel as good as when a business owner appreciates my patronage, whether in a restaurant or another type of business. It is always pono to treat customers with respect, to be polite, and to serve them as you would wish to be served yourself. That is always the right thing to do, and the key to any successful business.

At the end of the day, what I remember most about my professional training as a waiter was how to best serve others, a core principle of pono. Just imagine a world where all people were treated like customers in a five-star restaurant. How *right* would it be to actually care about another's comfort, another's needs, another's satisfaction – without any thought of personal or financial gain on our part? Only by living pono will one ever experience that kind of level of personal reward, when service to others occurs naturally in our day-to-day lives - simply because it's the right thing to do, and for no other reason.

A Profile in Pono – Ron Panzo

No one understands the concept of pono in the workplace better than Ron Panzo, Managing Partner of Nalu's South Shore Grill in Kihei. Ron has been in the restaurant industry for more than 40 years, on both Maui and O'ahu, having been involved in such well-known establishments as Nick's Fishmarket in Waikiki, Sarrento's on the Beach in Kihei, and Lulu's in both Lahaina and Waikiki. As an avid surfer on Waikiki, a much younger Ron sacrificed surf time to observe his employer Nick Nickolas, owner of Nick's, run his business in the 1970s. Inspired by Nick's professional work ethic, Ron quickly moved his way through the ranks of the restaurant, all the way from dishwasher to general manager.

It was here, at Nick's, that Ron learned about pono in the workplace. "When I was a dishwasher or a busboy, at the age of 18 or 19 years old," he remembers, "when I would walk by a rubbish can I saw a wrapper on the side of the rubbish can, and I'd see three or four people walk by it, and I would look at it, and I'd try to walk by it, but I couldn't. I'd have to turn around and pick it up." Why? Because Ron understood, even at that young age, that picking up that wrapper, which was purposely ignored by all the other employees, was the right thing to do.

Nick's may have been where Ron learned about pono in the workplace, but the foundation of living pono is something he learned, as a child, from observing his parents. "It rubs off on you," says Ron. "I think I was very fortunate; I was real blessed. My mom and dad were the same way. They opened their homes to anybody. Going through that upbringing laid the foundation. You always had that foundation, that anchor. There's times now, especially at my age, you feel that when you try to live that way, to direct your life in that direction, you're honoring your mom and dad as well."

A big part of the "foundation" laid during Ron's upbringing was being raised in a Catholic household. Like many young Catholics, Ron rebelled until he got a little older and was better able to reflect upon his faith in God. "Something stuck," he says, "There was a connection. Pono, for me, has a lot to do with doing what's right and serving my higher power." Ron now had an extra incentive to do the right thing – pleasing God.

Reflecting back to the "wrapper story," Ron says, "What the Lord asks us is to live pono," he says. "I remember telling myself, or say in a little prayer inside, saying 'You know what, Lord, I'm doing this for you. I don't care if anybody else sees me doing it, I know you're watching me do this.' It's the little things that become habit-forming, and all of a sudden you're doing it, and it's not even a headache to pick up a wrapper because it's just second nature now. You don't want to compromise."

Those early life lessons, while working as a dishwasher at Nick's Fishmarket in Waikiki, paid off huge dividends for Ron as he went from those humble beginnings to being a veteran restaurateur on Maui. His business philosophy at Nalu's is summed up in the restaurant's motto – "Eat Live Pono." Says Ron, "With the restaurant, we were totally blessed. We weren't expecting to be this busy and I attribute that to living pono. It's not a choice. You can't say this salad is going to be pono, and this one's not going to be pono. Every one has got to be pono. You got to do it with love. It takes a form of love to be pono. You got to love what you do while you're doing it."

Hearing Ron discuss how important consistency is in both food preparation and presentation in the restaurant business reminded me of when I would train my wait staff, in the front of the house, at my restaurants in California. Anytime that I would walk by a table and see a misplaced wineglass, salad fork, or butter plate, I would point out to the waitperson responsible for setting the table that it takes just as long a time to place the individual pieces in their correct positions as it does to place them incorrectly. Ron's right. Thinking back, the waiters who always set their tables perfectly were the ones who most loved what they did. Their love of their job affected how much pono they put into their work.

Taking Pono to the Next Level

The life lessons that Ron Panzo learned from his parents' example, and over 40 years in the restaurant business, only set the stage for the quantum leap of faith Ron was about to discover about what *real* pono was all about. Nalu's had only been opened for four months when news of terrorist attacks in Paris, 7,400 miles away, was broadcast on the restaurant's television sets on November 13, 2015. While everyone watched the news in disbelief, Ron felt a calling deep inside of his being.

Two oceans and two continents away, the suffering of the Parisian people was viscerally felt by everyone. Ron's first inclination was that the people of Paris needed a hug. "We still could feel the pain," Ron remembers. "We wanted to do something for them, and what could we do? And the first thing we thought was, we'll send a lei. Let's send the world's largest lei."

"The next morning I woke up," Ron continues, "I never had this feeling before, but I had this burning fire in my chest. I've never felt that kind of compassion or that type of, like, I got to do this. I just started calling anybody. Within three hours we raised $2,000, we had a Facebook page started, a website started, and a poster for Paris. That's how pono is sometimes; it's bigger than us. Once you start it, it just sucks you in."

The Lei of Aloha

What followed, in rapid succession, was nothing short of a miracle. Fourteen truckloads of ti leaves were delivered to Nalu's, where over 200 volunteers worked from 8am-10pm, for three-and-a-half days, to complete a 300-pound lei measuring one-mile in length. It took seven containers to transport the "Lei for Paris," which was accompanied by Ron and a small group of fellow ambassadors of aloha and pono. United Airlines agreed to transport the lei to Paris free of charge.

Once in Paris, the eight sections of the lei were delivered to different memorial sites and hospitals of those affected by the terrorist attacks. For the 130 murdered innocents, and the 368 people injured, there is very little that a grieving world can do to try and make things *right* again for the people of Paris. But what the good, decent people of Maui did, in the City of Lights, was to bring some light and some pono, across two oceans and two continents, simply because it seemed that giving Parisians a hug was the right thing to do. "That's all a testimony of, I believe, living pono," says Ron. Right you are, Ron, and bless you and all involved in the Lei for Paris, for your unselfish compassion and love.

A mere seven months later, on June 12, 2016, the world was again shocked by another terrorist attack in a gay nightclub in Orlando, Florida. In this attack, 49 people were killed, and another 53 were wounded. Once again, Ron Panzo knew what he needed to do. Rallying many of the same volunteers who helped make the Lei for Paris, he set to work on replicating another mile-long Lei of Aloha for the people of Orlando. This time, the number of volunteers doubled to 400 people, who worked nonstop for four days to complete the lei.

The Orlando lei was divided into three sections comprised of 49 strands, each 49 feet long. In addition, the lei was adorned with 49 cowrie shells, each one inscribed with the name of a soul lost in the terrorist attack. The Lei of Aloha was delivered to three different memorials - one section in front of the Pulse nightclub to honor the victims who died there, another to the Orlando Regional Medical Center, in support of medical professionals and the wounded who were in their care, and the last section of the lei was displayed at the Dr. Phillips Center for the Performing Arts.

At the time, Ron summed up the *why* for making the lei for Orlando. "Even though we're 5,000 miles away and another huge ocean away, we feel the pain, we feel the shock," says Ron. "We just wanted to reach out and give Orlando a hug to remind people that there's way more good people out there than there are bad people." Obviously, Ron is a man who believes in giving hugs to those who need them most. First it was to the grieving people of Paris, and then to those mourning in Orlando. In both instances, the Lei of Aloha was the right thing to do. It represented a beautiful sign of compassion and love. It embodied the best in the human spirit. In other words, it demonstrated true pono.

Because of all the acrimony shown before, during, and after the Presidential Election of 2016, a Kihei Charter School chemistry teacher approached Ron about possibly making a half-mile-long Lei of Aloha to take to the Presidential Inauguration in Washington D. C. on January 20, 2017. The idea was to take five students to our nation's capital to help promote love and unity during this time of strong political division. The lei was not intended to be political in any way. The schoolteacher, John Fitzpatrick, told Ron that he felt it was "the right thing to do."

In order to cover expenses, a private donor anonymously gifted $15,000 to Kihei Charter School. The students were part of a national Close Up program that participated with 2,300 other students from around the country in mock debates and a mock Congress. The students also got to tour the Capitol Building, the Smithsonian Institute, all the monuments, and meet with their State Senators and Representatives. The lei was ultimately presented at the Martin Luther King, Jr. Memorial.

Connecting the Dots

When I asked Ron to summarize what pono meant to him personally, he replied, "I think pono is real simple. It starts by waking up in the morning and taking your first breath and go, 'Wow, thank you. Thank you.' Gratitude plays a big role. The more gratitude you have, the easier it is to be pono. I don't think you can have pono if you're not grateful." Starting with an attitude of gratitude, something shared by everyone who lives pono, the next step is to choose to live this way.

"It's a choice," says Ron. "You choose to live this way, or you don't choose to live this way. It's a conscious choice. And all throughout the day, from the time you get up in the morning until the time you go to bed, you've got all these choices going on. And so, to choose aloha, or to choose pono, is a continuing choice that you decide to do all day long. It doesn't just come by stumbling across it. And then it's a commitment. You've got to commit to it. Once you decide you want to be pono, you take on tasks whether they're difficult or they're easy – that's true pono."

What a great and accurate summation of what it means to truly practice *The Pono Principle*. It reminds me of the example I used earlier about how it takes the exact same amount of time, and effort, to correctly set a table as it does to incorrectly set it. So it is with living pono. It is just as easy for me to spend my day focused on doing the next *right* thing, as it is to focus on just doing the next *some* thing. There is no shortage of self-help books in the marketplace that advise readers on how to be more productive in their lives, but this may be the first book to help guide you to a more elevated state of productivity, where one's actions are intended to be mutually beneficial to everyone.

What if, starting tomorrow, every employee in the world went to work on time, gave 100% of themselves in their job performance, and never cheated or stole from their employers? What if every employee maintained a work ethic that made them feel like they were as invested in the success of their business as the owners of the company? How would that affect overall business performance, job satisfaction, productivity, profits for the company, and a sense of self-worth for all employees? In other words, what would the world be like if everyone put in an honest day's work for an honest day's pay? That's called instilling pono in the workplace.

When *The Pono Principle* is applied in the workplace, everyone benefits – business owners, employees and, especially, the customer. Pono in the workplace is the ultimate example of what a win-win-win situation looks like. If everyone in a business transaction is focused on doing the right thing, then everyone wins. It's really that simple.

We Aim to Please

Is it just me, or has the quality of customer service declined over the last several decades? Mind you, I'm old enough to remember the days of my youth when my father could pull into a filling station and an army of uniformed attendants would attack our car like a pit stop crew at the Indy 500. While one attendant started filling the gas tank, another was already under the hood checking the oil level, and yet another would be cleaning the windshield with a squeegee. Oh, and there was also the attendant who was checking the tire pressure while Dad sat in the driver's seat smoking his pipe.

Granted, that level of customer service ran out of gas by the end of the 1950s, and was never to be seen again. Today, when I pull up to a self-serve gas pump, I realize that I am completely on my own with regards to servicing my car's needs. Even though I can see someone sitting inside the mini-mart, the only service he or she is interested in supplying me is if I need a receipt for my gas, or a bag of Doritos. In many ways, the complete disappearance of customer service once found at filling stations is also reflected in most other American businesses today.

Few things in this world exemplify the practice of pono more than this thing called customer service. If you are lucky enough to experience first-rate customer service today, you feel like telling that individual's supervisor that you're not hanging up the phone until you know that he has given that outstanding employee a pay raise - and a corporate car. Conversely, if you have had to suffer, as many of us do these days, with some kind of I-don't-give-a-rip customer service representative, you may be more prone to wanting to order an airstrike on that employee's work cubicle (whether it's somewhere in India or in Scottsdale, Arizona). I believe that all consumers should be able to expect to be treated with courtesy and respect, as though their patronage was the most important thing to the people they are doing business with.

Certainly, any outstanding employee or customer service representative, who aims to please the customer, is someone who is demonstrating true pono in the workplace. By putting the customer first (something most businesses used to pride themselves in doing), today's quality service employees do right by their customers by making them feel like their business is valued, and that they appreciate these valued customers for spending their hard-earned money for their services. Only in this type of win-win-win business environment, is pono clearly demonstrated, and fully realized.

A Pono Life Lesson

My first exposure to the restaurant business was helping Monroe wash dishes in the kitchen of my mother's restaurant in Englewood, Colorado, in 1959. I was 6 years old and Monroe was the first black man I ever knew. My parents had just moved from Miami, Florida, to Colorado simply because my Mom happened to be going through *Volume 7 (Civil List to Coronium)* of our *Encyclopedia Americana* one day, and liked the pictures she saw of Colorado. True story. Within six months, our family moved to

Denver, Mom opened her restaurant, Mom went out of business, and we moved back to Miami.

You see, as hard as the restaurant business is for those who have years of experience in the industry, it's complete suicide for someone who was a banker's personal secretary only six months earlier, but thought that it might be fun to own a restaurant in a Denver suburb. Once Mom's employees realized that she was clueless on how to run her business, several of them started to steal her blind. Cash from the register was always short, drinks were regularly being comped by bartenders, and food inventory would constantly go missing. Simply put, there were more steaks and lobsters going out the back door, with the employees, than there were customers coming in the front door.

As memory serves me, it was Mom's dishwasher, Monroe, who alerted her that her employees were stealing food on a regular basis. Of course, this crushed my mother on a multitude of levels, but mostly because my mother had such devout faith in the inherent goodness in people. How could they do this to her? It just wasn't right.

Certainly, what the dishonest employees at my mother's restaurant did was the complete opposite of pono. They were thieves who took advantage of a very trusting, albeit naïve, person who probably should not have gotten into the restaurant business in the first place - but, most certainly, didn't deserve to be put out of business because of their wrongful actions. Knowing my mother, I'm sure that her takeaway memory from that experience was that she was lucky to have an honest dishwasher work for her named Monroe.

But how different were my mother's dishonest employees from you and me? How many times have employees justified stealing from their employers because they felt they were being taken advantage of, that they weren't being paid enough, or that their bosses were so wealthy that it wouldn't upset their lifestyles? How many employees have rationalized that, if their bosses weren't able to catch them stealing, that they deserved to be ripped off? How many salespeople, with corporate expense accounts, have padded their expense reports with personal items and expenses? How many used the corporate gas card to fill up their personal vehicles? How many office workers think nothing of taking office supplies home from their workplace? How many bartenders pick up the cash left behind by a customer for his drinks, only to put it in their tip jars?

At one time or another, I can honestly admit that I have committed several of these dishonest deeds myself. Every time that I ever helped myself to some wine, or other alcoholic beverage, while working as a waiter, I was stealing from my employer. And when other fellow waiters followed my example, by drinking mistakes from the bar or having some wine during their shifts, how were we, collectively, contributing to the detriment of our employer's bottom line? Having seen the anguish that my mother went through because her dishonest staff stole from her, whatever their rationalization, fills me with personal shame because I was guilty of the same sin and unlawful act.

That was certainly a dark chapter in my life that I thank God everyday I learned from and have never repeated. Had I been practicing *The Pono Principle* as a much younger man, those embarrassing acts would never have happened in my life, nor in the lives of those employers I so disappointed because of my dishonesty. The life lesson I learned very clearly is that it is never too late, or too early, to start living pono from this day forward - regardless of what sins you have committed in your past.

End Two-
Party System

De-Polarize
Electorate

Create
Third Force

Civility Restored

Chapter 6

Pono In Politics

*Unless it is politically profitable for the wrong people to do
the right thing, the right people will not do the right thing
either, or it they try, they will shortly be out of office.*
                                                    - Milton Friedman

In the autumn of 1974, I was a student at Michigan State
University and had the opportunity to spend an evening with
Stephen Stills, after he had finished doing a benefit concert for a
local congressional candidate, Bob Carr. It's a rather long, elaborate
tale so I won't go into minute detail. Simply put, I followed Stephen
into his dressing room, gave him a Martin guitar t-shirt, met Roger
McGuinn of The Byrds, and was then invited to join his entourage
as we drove to Carr's campaign headquarters in Lansing. Once
there, Stephen recorded some radio spots for the campaigning
congressman. When he finished, he turned to me and said, "You're
a student here, right? Where's a good place to go get a drink?" "I
know just the place," I said. "I'll take you there."

Stephen and I walked to a local bar in the company of Stephen's
companion, Bob. Once seated, we ordered drinks and I proceeded
to ask Stephen questions as though I were a writer for *Rolling Stone*
magazine. Stephen talked a lot about the Democratic Party as being
the only beacon of enlightenment in the political spectrum, and
I challenged him on that. Mind you, I was merely a 21-year-old
college student, had only voted in one presidential election, and was
politically naïve enough to assume that the most important feature
about political candidates was their character, not their political

party. Stephen adamantly disagreed. He argued that it was the party, not the individual, which mattered most to him.

Since that day, I have maintained my naïve notion that our republic, the United States of America, is only great when great leaders, not great political parties, lead it. Although I refuse to pigeonhole my political thinking by self-identifying as either a Republican or Democrat, I do tend to adhere far more to the *republican* (small *r*) political principles put forth during our nation's inception. Some would say that makes me a *conservative* rather than a *liberal* or *progressive.* For the record, whenever I have taken political quizzes on the Internet, I always score heavily Libertarian. While I wholeheartedly support maximum liberty in both personal and economic matters, advocate a much smaller government, support the free market, embrace individual responsibility, oppose government bureaucracy and taxes, promote private charity, and tolerate diverse lifestyles, I don't blindly follow the libertarian mode of thought wherever it leads. I do reserve certain concerns about the practicality of some of the more extreme libertarian positions.

A Constitutional Patriot's Litmus Test

It is clearly evident that the vast majority of Americans identify themselves with a particular political party. If the words Republican or Democrat are not used, most will say that their political views are either conservative or liberal. Still others, who might not wish to attach a politically defining noun or adjective to themselves, will opt for a verb to describe their views by saying that they either lean right or left. And then there are those centrists, moderates, or independents, whose views occupy the middle ground between the two extremes.

The problem that I see in using these political terms to identify ourselves and others is that their definitions are often very broad and, worse, can change over the years. Perspective is everything when one uses terms like *conservative* or *liberal,* for example. Even within one's own political party, individuals will argue that so-and-so is not conservative enough or, perhaps, is *too* liberal. I have also seen where someone is accused of not being a *true* conservative (e.g. a neoconservative) for this or that reason.

Not only does general political identification hinder people from being able to properly capsulize their most basic political views in a meaningful way, but they also set themselves up for being the target of a myriad of false-representations when challenged by the opposing political view. Since no one, these days, can agree as to what defines any of the political parties, no one has a clear idea as to what our politicians believe in or support. Which leaves us with campaign dog-and-pony shows, smoke and mirrors, lots of tap dancing, and shameless pandering to individual audiences and supporters.

Today's political climate is rife with little more than party talking points, more intent on brainwashing party members than on supplying them with substantive information to help them vote their consciences. Never have I seen more vitriolic crossfire from both political camps, nor such a lack of tolerance for opposing political ideas among the citizenry of our nation. Because of these modern propaganda techniques, we may be in the midst of having the largest ill-informed electorate ever. Whether one watches man-on-the-street interviews, where clueless voters have no idea who the candidates even are (yet alone what issues they endorse), or one reads moronic Letters to the Editor from voters who can only regurgitate the propaganda talking points put forth by their party, the takeaway is the same – it's a sad day for America.

The last time I checked, I never took a pledge of allegiance to any one political party. I did, however, voluntarily take the following oath when I enlisted in the United States Army, at the age of 18:

> *I do solemnly swear that I will support and defend the Constitution of the United States against all enemies, foreign and domestic; that I will bear true faith and allegiance to the same . . . So help me God.*

There is no duration period on the oath of enlistment - it is indeterminate. Which means that, over four decades later, I still hold to that oath with every fiber of my being. I am an American patriot because I swore that I would be nothing less. I took a solemn vow that I would defend our *Constitution,* with my life, against anyone. And "anyone" means *anyone* – a foreign army, terrorists, or even subversive groups within our own country – *"all* enemies, foreign *and* domestic."

Because of the fact that everything I value about America is contained in our *United States Constitution,* when asked about my personal political views, I simply identify myself as a Constitutional Patriot. Unlike any other political party member, it is very easy for me to clearly define my political views. I simply point to the three parchments hanging on my wall – the *Declaration of Independence,* the *Constitution,* and the *Bill of Rights* – and tell people that everything I believe in, concerning the United States, is written upon those three documents.

This has become my new political litmus test. When anyone, whether it's a friend, someone on the street, or a political fundraiser on the phone, asks me whom I'm voting for in an upcoming election, I just say that I am a Constitutional Patriot, and then pause. Without fail, the response is always the same, "Oh, so you're voting for *that* guy." How sad that the whole world knows whom an American patriot would undoubtedly vote for, and yet would, themselves, consider voting for the other candidate. What does that say about the state of our country, our political candidates, or the multitude of clueless, ill-informed voters who have no inkling as to the magnitude of what's at stake in our election process?

Where are our Constitutional Patriots? For the sake of our great republic, my fervent prayer is that they stand up and be counted.

An Independent Third Force

My personal feeling is that the biggest problem with today's political climate in America rests in our two-party system. The extreme polarity of political views coming from both the Democratic and Republican parties has created an atmosphere where neither party is even willing to tolerate it's opponent's positions on anything. Simply put, our politics today have devolved into mere divisiveness and partisanship. It seems to me that the only thing that the two power-hungry political parties can agree upon is that there is no room for a third-party in the political arena. Put a Libertarian or Independent candidate on any ballot and watch how quickly a Democratic-Republican coalition will take up arms to obliterate said third-party candidate. The only thing that scares our two-party system worse than each other is the very notion that a viable, challenging third political party might rise up in America.

What we need is not another political third-party, but an independent political *third force*. Now, when I refer to a political third force I'm not necessarily referring to a political third-party (e.g. Green Party or Constitution Party). What I mean to say is that, for far too long, we have relegated American politics to being a binary system of paired opposites – Republicans vs. Democrats, conservatism vs. liberalism, right vs. left. This has created a place of *two-ness* in opposition, like we see in competitive sports. We treat our elections like football games between two opposing teams where only one can be victorious. Like rabid fans at a game, we wholeheartedly cheer for our team while we boo, cuss, and denigrate the opposing team. Of course, the Super Bowl of our electoral process is the Presidential Election every four years.

Because of this binary win/lose mentality Americans have towards two-party political elections, we have lost much of our political objectivity and have, instead, become a bunch of Kool-Aid drinkers for one party or the other. Perhaps the most glaring development over the years has been an electorate that is increasingly more in your face when their party wins an election while, conversely, becoming completely unhinged when they lose one. Our two-party American voters seem to have lost the civility to be either gracious winners *or* losers.

The other very noticeable political dynamic seen today is the extent to which party apologists will go to cover up the failures, lies, and blatant hypocrisy, demonstrated by their party and/or politicians. It's one thing for an individual politician to get caught, red-handed, telling a lie to the world (e.g. " I did not have sexual relations with that woman, Miss Lewinsky"), but what does it tell you about everyone else who defends and/or excuses that lie? Where's *their* integrity? Probably in the same place as the person telling the lie – in that sanctuary of political justification and rationalization where they will sanction any, and all, behavior that furthers their shared political ideology. Also, observe how these same diehard party apologists will try to make *you* feel like you are somehow complicit in some kind of conspiracy to catch the guy with his pants down – when only *he* is responsible for having his pants down in the first place.

But political apologists have now waged all out war on anyone who so much as questions their party politics. Their new strategy is to label party-identified deplorables as ever so many haters, racists, misogynists, homophobes, xenophobes, white supremacists, Nazis, and/or fascists. Interestingly, seldom is any individual branded with only one or two of these slanderous epithets – if an apologist perceives you as a threat, prepare to be garlanded with all of them, all at once. It's just easier for them to try to shame half of the American populace by unleashing a shotgun blast of hate-filled vitriol than to engage in open public discourse. Such is the state of our political landscape today.

Perhaps the only thing more egregious, and hypocritical, than the pervasive political infighting that takes place between the Democrats and Republicans is when there is the same type of infighting displayed, within each of the two parties, during primary elections. Case in point: Of the 17 major Republican presidential candidates, who relentlessly slung mud and insults at each other throughout the 2016 Primary Election, two ended up being appointed to the incoming President's cabinet. One day "Candidate"

Trump is calling his Republican challengers all kinds of demeaning names while, the next day, "President" Trump appoints two of these men as Secretaries of the Departments of Energy and Housing & Urban Development. It appears that politics, even within one's own party, seems to make for some fickle friends.

I seriously don't think we have seen such contentious political infighting since the American Civil War, a time in our history when the most monumental political debate sadly demonstrated how our two political parties could only see their world as "black and white." A century and a half later, the alienation and polarization shown in our modern-day political scene is still reprehensible at its core. The binary system of political thought – black and white, as in this example – is at the root of our country's political woes. What to do?

Pono to the Rescue

In a court of law, what kind of judicial resolution could one expect to see if a verdict relied solely on the conflicting testimonies of defendants and plaintiffs? On one hand, you have a prosecuting attorney accusing a man of being guilty of a crime, while a defense attorney is making a case that his client is completely innocent of said crime. Which is it, guilty or innocent? These are purely binary choices based only upon binary testimonies. Truly, there can be no judicial resolution in such a limited binary system.

Since the days of King Solomon, the only way to guarantee a just resolution in a court of law was by adding a third force – a third party without a "dog in the fight" – to weigh the evidence and determine an impartial verdict. That "third force" was called a judge, a person who serves as the necessary reconciling mediator between these polar opposite courtroom representatives. The judge becomes the objective third force who neutralizes the other two subjective forces in order to arrive at a new realm of possibility (i.e.

resolution), one that would be unattainable in a binary system. That "new realm of possibility" is where one finds pono.

In like manner, pono in politics can never be found in a political arena limited to only two diametrically opposing forces like the Democrats and Republicans. Only when a compassionately indifferent, independent third force is introduced to objectively neutralize the polarized political views of the binary two-party system (i.e. the *prison* of only two ideas), will we ever find pono in politics. That third force will redeem each of the two parties' positions while giving everyone a valuable role to play in the creation of something genuinely new, a fourth possibility – pono in politics. But what is that third force that can permanently destroy the political stalemate that exists in today's Congress? What is it that has the power to throw a bucket of cold water on the vitriolic, divisive rhetoric and behavior demonstrated by the Kool-Aid drinkers on both the left and right? The answer is an informed, objective electorate – patriotic Americans who understand that our country is best when we learn how to marry, not separate, the most virtuous values from both liberal and conservative circles, and unleash them, not only for the betterment of our citizenry, but for all the world.

A Calm in the Eye of the Storm

As I have pointed out, and demonstrated, by other life lessons I have learned, oftentimes it takes a tragedy to, ultimately, bring out the best in us. Cases in point are the recent hurricanes Harvey and Irma that absolutely devastated the States of Texas and Florida. Watching the news reporting on these back-to-back natural disasters reminded me of hunkering down at my grandparent's house in Miami, during Hurricane Donna, in 1960. I was only seven years old, but I vividly remember the howling winds blowing on the other side of the plywood-covered windows and doors. The only thing that stifled whatever fears I had at the time was the fact that the external surrounding hurricane did little to dampen the internal surroundings of my grandparent's home – where I played with my cousins on the floor while the rest of my family prayed and kept calm.

To witness the level of damage done by the extreme high winds and flooding, to the good people of Texas and Florida, ended up saying more about *their* character and resolve than anything else. What these two natural disasters proved to the world is that we *are* a good people at our core, that we can take whatever life throws at us, and still stand united together in comforting and assisting each other, determined to rebuild our lives and carry on. What was most evident, amid the destruction of personal property, and the flooded streets, homes and businesses, is that nobody cared about their neighbors' race, creed, sexual orientation, or political affiliation – all of us were simply fellow human beings in need of help.

Regardless of how much political vitriol was being tossed around by the media *before* Harvey and Irma, even the most avid Trump-haters on cable news found the human decency to focus on the real news of the human tragedy playing out before our nation's eyes. All of a sudden, President Trump's "tweets" were not the main story of the day – good, decent Americans practicing pono *was*. In the midst of *real* national devastation, that was palpable to the entire world, we saw our citizens, our first responders, and our President, do what was right under the extreme circumstances facing them. What we witnessed was *The Pono Principle* in action, neighbors rescuing neighbors, strangers helping strangers, individuals focused on one thing, and one thing only – doing the next right thing. What a blessing to witness.

A Pono Life Lesson

The 1980 U. S. Presidential Election pitted incumbent President Jimmy Carter against former California Governor Ronald Reagan. At that time, my wife and I had only been married two years, so this was the first election in which we voted as a couple. Neither my wife nor I were very politically savvy in those early days of our marriage, but we certainly planned on voting in the upcoming election between Carter and Reagan. Although both my wife and I grew up in fairly conservative households, we were certainly aware of, and sympathetic towards, some of the liberal views espoused by many within our "Woodstock Generation" - but not enough to just blow off Reagan as a right-wing nut job, as many of our generation did back then.

Enter Albert Anthony Augustitus, a bearded 63-year-old man who used to park his truck on the side of Highway 1 in Carmel, California, and wave an American flag at passersby. Albert wore a hard hat and a sandwich board urging motorists to write him in as an Independent candidate in the upcoming presidential election. "Triple A, All the Way" was his campaign slogan. Oftentimes, we would see him handing out apples to passing motorists, or 1-gallon plastic containers of milk. His truck was covered with numerous political and religious slogans, mostly promoting a "God and Country" vision for America.

I don't remember too many people back then who were all that excited about the job performance of Jimmy Carter during his first term as President, and many of our young friends were petrified that if Ronald Reagan were elected President he would bring us to the brink of nuclear war with the Soviet Union. So, who to vote for? Should we even consider the possibility of voting for an Independent candidate for President of the United States, or would that be an act of throwing our vote away? What's the right thing to do when you aren't very excited, or won over, by the two candidates chosen by their respective political parties? After all, isn't voting one's conscience the ultimate act of doing the right thing (in spite of what Stephen Stills may believe)?

I can vividly remember going to our designated polling location and not feeling comfortable with either of the two-party choices for President of the United States. As I stood in my voting booth, unsure of the right choice to cast my vote for, my wife leaned over from her adjoining booth and asked me, "How do you spell 'Augustitus'?" Immediately, my mind flashed to this grey-bearded, patriotic World War Two Army veteran standing on the side of the road, handing out food to passersby, while waving the American flag, and I knew what I had to do.

At no time since that 1980 Presidential Election have I ever felt more privileged to exercise my Constitutional right to vote. Even then, all those many years ago, I felt that the two-party system was failing America. Rather than accepting the limited views of two diametrically opposing political ideologies, my wife and I chose to vote for an independent third political force. We chose to cast our votes for a man whom we could physically observe doing what he believed in his heart to be the right thing to do, and for the right reasons - all the while proclaiming his vision for America in the words he had inscribed on his sandwich board and the sides of his truck.

Two years later, in 1982, Albert Anthony Augustitus ran for Governor of the State of California, as an Independent, an election in which he received nine votes. I have little doubt that two of those votes came from my wife and me.

Clean Land

Clean Sea

Clean Air

A Pono World

Chapter 7

Pono And The Environment

You got to be pono. You must have done the rightful thing on the land.
- Kimokeo Kapahulehua

How much daily thought do we really give to how our actions affect the world around us? Are most of us so egocentric that we think that it is acceptable to litter, waste water, or not completely extinguish a smoldering campfire in the woods? At what point do we disregard that voice in our head that says, "Tossing that gum wrapper on the sidewalk is not good for the environment?" I would argue that most of us, to some degree and at some time, have been guilty of littering, not recycling our waste, and being wasteful with our natural resources. More importantly, I would further argue that somewhere inside of us we knew that those actions were inherently wrong.

Expanding on these small, environmentally unfriendly decisions we make as individual people, consider how whole committees of people making decisions about land use, water and air pollution, and protection of endangered species further emphasize the importance of right thinking and right actions (i.e. pono). None of us live in an insulated bubble. Figuratively speaking, we all drink from the same well, we all breathe the same air, and we all swim in the same ocean. Therefore, we must begin to consider how our personal day-to-day decisions, however small, can truly make profound differences (positively or negatively) with regards to the world that we all share together.

As I am writing these words, a 140-year industry has just closed down on the last sugar-producing island in Hawaii - Maui. No more smoke billowing out of the sugar factory chimneys, no more seasonal cane burning producing black snow across south Maui, and no more water being diverted to the cane fields. These environmental plusses are currently being weighed against the potential backlash of mass unemployment, future agricultural use of fallow sugar cane fields, and whether or not to use the land for commercial or residential use.

How best to transition Maui's now fallow sugar cane fields for future use will rely heavily on the amount of pono demonstrated in the decision-making process over the next weeks, months, and years. The 36,000 acres of former sugar land on Maui is being diversified and repurposed. Some proposed uses include diversified agriculture, biodiesel-producing tree orchards, coffee and cacao crops, and livestock-irrigated pastures. Some of the land has already been zoned for commercial development, and other areas will be difficult to reutilize because it has sat fallow for so long. A new 9-acre shopping center is currently being developed in Kahului.

Also at issue, is the challenge some taro farmers are now facing regarding what was a 100-year-old water diversion supply from East Maui to their fields in Upcountry and Central Maui. Alexander & Baldwin (A&B), the owners of the 36,000 acres in question, faces the Herculean task of doing what is pono for the land, and its people. When A&B shut down Hawaiian Commercial & Sugar Company (HC&S) at the end of 2016, over 600 members of its workforce were forced to find other jobs. The hope is that many of the ex-HC&S workers will be absorbed into the future agricultural projects proposed.

A Profile in Pono - Kimokeo Kapahulehua

A cultural icon here on Maui, and throughout the Hawaiian island chain, Kimokeo Kapahulehua, is a 21st Century Hawaiian cultural warrior fighting to preserve the traditions, core values, and history that are uniquely associated with this Pacific island paradise. Much has been written about Kimokeo's contributions throughout the years with regards to his sense of *kuleana* (a sacred responsibility) in seeing to it that there remains a perpetuation of the Hawaiian culture for future generations to experience and learn from. Whether it is the preservation of the Hawaiian language, its canoe culture, the restoration of ancient fishponds, or the preservation and sustainability of its agricultural land, Kimokeo is tireless in his determination to do what is pono (right) for the *āina* (land) and her *kama'āina* (people of the land).

Sitting on a bench, overlooking Maluaka Beach, on a beautiful Makena morning, I asked 69-year-old Kimokeo how important the principle of pono has been in his life. "Probably, I don't look at pono," he began, "I think pono looks at me. I don't think you can see pono, I think you have to live pono. I think it is something that we all have, and we all inherit it. We inherit pono by doing all the things that we should do. Pono should be an example to all the family, the youngest child. That is part of pono, raising a child, to do what you should do as a living person, not to do it because you learn it, or been told, or been educated."

With regards to the environment, a subject he has championed for his entire life, Kimokeo said, "So, how are we pono? And how are we applying it to take care of the people of the heaven, the ocean, and the land? That's what you call living pono. Why should we be educated to keep the air clean, the ocean clean, and the land clean? That should be pono. I find pono is a living part of my life." As it turns out, Kimokeo's cultural philosophy is entirely in sync with the Hawaii State motto: *Ua Mau ke Ea o ka 'Āina i ka Pono* ("The life of the land is perpetuated in righteousness").

Kimokeo's father, uncle, grandmother, mother and aunts showed him the way to the ocean, the way to the land. They taught him the philosophy of *mālama honua* – take care of the land, and the land will take care of you. His father and uncle were deep-sea divers who showed him where to go, what to take, what not to take, and how much to take. "Examples are a good thing," Kimokeo says, "but now we got an example, now we got to live pono."

As we observed the distant outrigger canoes that were returning from the Molokini Challenge, we acknowledged we were "lucky we live Maui." I couldn't help but think of Robert Browning's line: "God's in His heaven - All's right with the world!" Of course, I realized that the Hawaiian translation would be, "All's pono with the world!" Kimokeo expressed our feelings this way, "I think every sunrise, and every sunset is pono. And if you can view it like we can do on Maui, that's super-pono."

Kimokeo expanded his definition of pono by adding, "I think, for me, pono is the truth, the way it should be, and the way it should be done. Everyone's been taught that pono means to do it right, but recently, in the last 20 years, I think it's about truth. Pono is the truth. Pono is a shared plan, examples of doing the right thing, living it, breathing it, being part of your life." I couldn't agree more that the practice of doing the right thing in all things (i.e. pono) may be one of the greatest truths I have discovered in life.

But it is as a respected *kupuna* (elder), who has accepted his responsibility *(kuleana)* as a cultural leader, where Kimokeo bests describes how pono is vital to the future of Maui, and to the preservation of ancient Hawaiian culture. "Anyone who can preserve, perpetuate, and educate culture is a rich, rich source. A hundred years from today, if we have language schools teaching our children language, doing canoe, hula dancing - all of this that we keep a hundred years later – that's going to be a 'Century of Pono.'"

For over 10 years, Kimokeo has worked tirelessly on the restoration of the Ko'ie'ie Fishpond in Kihei. Legend has it that ancient *menehune* (race of small people) built the original fishpond within one night. It was later rebuilt in the 1500s, but after centuries of storm surges and neglect, the fishpond was in grave disrepair. Since 2005, restoration of the fishpond began in earnest, and is still being worked on today, spearheaded by a fishpond restoration association ('Ao'ao O Na Loko I'a O Maui), of which Kimokeo is president. Today, during low tide, most of the hard work put in by an army of volunteers, who have labored for many years, is visible – the fishpond's 1,100-foot semicircular rock wall.

To Kimokeo, the revitalizing of the fishpond's rock wall is a way of revitalizing his Hawaiian culture. In ancient times, if a fishpond needed to be repaired, the entire community was summoned to do their share of work. With every heavy stone that is added to the wall by today's community of volunteers (many of whom are only visitors to Maui), Kimokeo's dream of restoring and preserving the traditions of ancient Hawaiian culture becomes more of a reality. And at the heart of that reality is the spirit of pono.

Tropical Paradise Pollution

Most people would probably assume that an island like Maui would naturally be more immune to the kind of air, noise, and land pollution that is more prevalent in more industrial areas of the world - such is not the case. Although humans are not responsible for the volcanic smog (VOG) that blows over from the Big Island and pollutes our air from time to time, humans are indeed responsible for dumping waste and litter from their boats into our waters, while also leaving our beaches littered with their discarded refuse. Marine debris or trash is one of the biggest environmental threats since much of the debris is comprised of plastics and other materials that resist natural degradation.

Every single day, 3-5 million gallons of wastewater are dumped into the ground, through injection wells, at a facility in Lahaina. Naturally, this causes wastewater to end up in the ocean, which adversely affects marine life, fragile coral reefs, and more than 7,000 marine life forms (25% of which are indigenous to the Hawaiian Islands). This daily activity, coupled with the pesticide and feces-laden runoff that flushes into the ocean, has contributed to causing bacterial infectious diseases like Staphylococcus and Streptococcus. Over the years that I have lived here, I have caught both staph and strep infections just by swimming in the ocean with nothing more than the most minuscule of cuts on my legs.

Coral bleaching is another noticeable environmental problem here on Maui. Some attribute it solely to an increase in ocean temperature. Scientists from the Nature Conservancy have recently stated that nearly half of Hawaii's coral reefs were bleached due to the heat waves in 2014 and 2015. Others will argue that much of coral bleaching is due to several genotoxic chemicals (oxybenzone being the main culprit), found in sunscreen lotions and sprays, which can damage a coral's DNA, and cause a disruption in its ability to develop and reproduce. While bleached coral often recovers slowly over time, multiple years of bleaching weakens the organisms and increases the risk of death. It is important to remember that coral reefs are among the most biologically diverse ecosystems in the world. Covering less than 1% of the ocean's floor, they are home to nearly one million species of fish, invertebrates, and algae. Coral reefs also shelter the land from storm surges and rising sea levels.

The "Polar" Global Warming Duality

Global warming believer? Global warming denier? Which are you? You realize that you're only given those two choices, so you had better pick one and stand by the talking point propaganda of those zealots who insist that this is a war between two opposing armies, one very virtuous, and the other the spawn of Satan. Let me guess which one you will be prone to gravitate towards, even if you don't know the difference between a tsunami and a can of Simoniz car wax. The heated discussion about, and continuous flame-fanning of, global warming is one of many political creations necessary to keep the electorate fired up as they sit in their respective boxing corners, determined to knock out their opponent, yet totally confused as to why they are in the ring to begin with.

Perhaps no modern-day political football has been more overinflated, conflated, and piously flatulated out of the mouths of *expert* ex-Vice Presidents and *professional* pro-climate change advocates than global warming. That's not to say that I don't agree with much of the scientific evidence that points in that direction. What I do have a major problem with is how scientific research is manipulated, exaggerated, or flat out lied about, by politicians for the sole purpose of attracting voters to their party's ideological position on climate change, regardless of what is the truth. And mind you, in a country where the political power has been relegated to only two political parties, "We the People" are thus relegated to supporting only one of two opposing views on the subject – that which our party has drilled into our scientifically ignorant heads.

Of course, the pono way of addressing the subject of global warming and/or climate change is to move beyond the limitations of the binary, dualistic opposing views, and seek the truth of the matter in a third field of possibility. Again, a third way is not the same thing as a mid-point, or compromise, between two binary views. What if both opposing views are idiotic? You certainly don't want to come to conclusions based solely on compromises between two stupid ideas or proposed solutions. I have found that the answer is almost always outside of dualistic thinking – it lies in a third way which I call the right (pono) decision. I'll give you an example.

As stated, so much of what people believe about global warming is what they have been indoctrinated to believe from the propaganda put out by whichever political party they align with. Seriously, how many people have actually taken the time to study up on what causes climate change? All they really know is that, if they belong to one political party, they are supposed to believe in the further exploration, and extraction, of fossil fuels. If they belong to the other team, then they're supposed to believe that those fossil fuel people are the same thing as Neanderthals. "Why don't those idiots know that the answer lies in electric cars, wind turbines, and solar panels?"

they might ask. "Certainly, the answer must be that we are so much more intelligent than they." And so goes the global warming debate.

Yet, having just witnessed the devastation leveled upon Texas and Florida during Hurricanes Harvey and Irma, one stark reality hit me like a two-by-four violently blown through the windshield of my car. In the midst of both of those horrific storms, electricity was the first thing to go. Millions of Americans had no power for many days as the hurricanes slowly swept across their States. That is, with the exception of the Neanderthals who had stored gasoline so as to power their generators at home, and to power their boats that they used to help rescue their neighbors. Electric cars, wind turbines, and solar panels were as useless to them, at that crucial time, as electric toothbrushes.

You see, the first thing that many people need to realize is that they have allowed themselves to be puppets of their political parties. Rather than using their own common sense and personal knowledge concerning environmental issues, they just align themselves with whatever talking points are pumped out by their party. I firmly believe that most people would agree that we need a multitude of energy sources to run efficiently, that pollution is never a good thing, that everyone should drink clean water, and that we must keep our planet clear of debris and litter. There lies the third way of finding the answers to global warming and climate change. When we refuse to align ourselves to opposing dualistic views, and seek unbiased truth from unbiased sources, we find the answers. That's the pono way.

A Pono Life Lesson

Several weeks ago, as I was doing my morning beachwalk, I noticed a bottle cap, face up, on the edge of the pathway. Since I was on my way to the gym, and in a hurry, I decided to ignore picking it up, but promised myself that I would retrieve it on my return. When I got to the gym, I told the gym attendant about my missed opportunity to take a pono action step, in the moment, when I first laid eyes on the discarded bottle cap. What if someone were to cut the bottom of his or her foot on it because I didn't pick it up? What if it's a little boy or girl? My shame for not practicing pono, at the moment I was in a position to do just that, troubled my conscience.

But then, a more troubling thought entered my mind. Would anyone else walking along the beachwalk pick up that bottle cap between now and when I pass by there in several hours? I'm embarrassed to say that my first inclination was that no one would, even if they saw it lying there. Such was my lack of faith in my fellow man. "I've got five bucks," I said to the attendant, "that says that that bottle cap is still lying there when I return to that spot." Talk about a very negative preconception, and certainly not a pono attitude.

How ashamed I was, several hours later, to find that the bottle cap had been picked up. How could I so overlook the good in others by assuming that no one else would be conscientious enough to pick it up? Whether it was a groundskeeper, or a tourist, or a passing local, someone bent over and picked up that bottle cap – something I didn't do myself when given the opportunity. Double shame. Lesson learned.

Several days ago, on the same walk, I was talking with a friend of mine when I noticed a discarded cigarette butt on the pathway. Immediately, I had a flashback to my time in the Army when we used to have morning police calls, where we would line up in formation and walk through a designated area, picking up cigarette butts and any other litter we found. I also flashbacked on the bottle cap incident from the week before. But this time, with absolutely no hesitation whatsoever, I bent over and picked up the butt, and held it in my hand until we came upon a trash container into which I deposited said butt. This time I chose to take a pono action step - and the world had one less cigarette butt to concern itself with.

These two incidents may sound very trivial to some, but I believe it is this type of *Other Consciousness* where pono oftentimes begins. What I decided to do that day was to never again underestimate the good in others – ever. I also resolved to never again assume that I was the only environmentally conscientious person in the world just because some other people might litter. I also promised myself that I would never again miss an opportunity to remove a broken piece of glass, a nail, or anything else (like a bottle cap) that could cause damage to someone's bare foot or car tire. Lastly, I joined a volunteer cleanup crew that picks up litter on the beaches.

If not me, who?

Chapter 8

Living Pono

Living pono benefits everybody.

- Jason Scott Lee

Perhaps the easiest way to figure out whether or not you are living pono is to examine your actions to see if, first of all, they are the right thing to do, whether they only benefit you, and to what degree do they benefit others and the environment. Once you have made a habit of asking yourself, "What is the next right thing I could be doing," and then actually doing that right thing, can it be said that you are truly living pono. Until then, you are merely living life; you are not focused on living a life of higher purpose and mutual concern.

The simple truth is that we are all creatures of habit. And if we are in the habit of never asking ourselves whether our actions are *right,* whether they could be done better, or whether others will benefit from them, then *The Pono Principle* will open a whole new world to you. Once you begin to make a habit of incorporating pono into your daily decision-making process, your sense of purpose will skyrocket. You will start to witness the overwhelming positive effects of right thinking put into action, and you will soon discover that pono will become its own habitual motivator for you to take further mutually beneficial actions. Over time, you won't even notice that both your decisions and actions have been influenced by a desire to do the right thing – you will just be in the habit of living pono each and every day.

I have been blessed to know many Hawaiian men and women who live pono on a daily basis, without any thought that there is any other way to live. It is how they were taught to live but, more importantly, it is how they were shown to live. I can honestly say that I, too, was shown how to live pono, primarily by the example of my father. Dad had a strong sense of right and wrong, he stood by his principles, and he had a strong faith in God. To such a man as he, pono was a quality that grew well in the soil of his being. He lived pono to the fullest.

Acting in the Present Moment

In Ralph Waldo Emerson's *Essays: First Series. Self-Reliance,* he says:

> *But man postpones or remembers; he does not live in the present, but with reverted eye laments the past, or, heedless of the riches that surround him, stands on tiptoe to foresee the future. He cannot be happy and strong until he too lives with nature in the present, above time.*[25]

Emerson states that man's timidity and shame do not allow him to live in perfect, timelessness like the roses that grow under his window. Unlike man, a rose's "nature is satisfied and it satisfies nature in all moments alike." The secret to the rose existing perfectly, "above time," is not simply in its existence, but in its action:

> *Before a leaf-bud has burst, its whole life acts; in the full-blown flower there is no more; in the leafless root there is no less.*[26]

So much is written today about simply living in the present, as though living, in and of itself, were the end goal. As a recovering alcoholic, I find that reasoning to be as much a half-truth as saying that the end goal to recovery is simply sobriety. Just staying sober for the rest of my life has absolutely nothing to do with the action steps

I need to take, each and every day, to be a better human being, to be the man God intended me to be. What benefit does a recovering alcoholic experience from sobriety if he spends his remaining years as a dry drunk, still stuck with all of his character defects and shortcomings? The key to a better life, therefore, is not in *living* in the present moment, but in *acting* in the present moment. Profound daily reminders, to act in the present moment, can be found in Henry Wadsworth Longfellow's *A Psalm of Life:*

> *Trust no Future, howe'er pleasant! Let the dead Past bury its dead! Act, – act in the living Present! Heart within, and God o'erhead!*[27]

Many people dwell on their past experiences out of a desire to relive, replay, or rehash either the splendor in the grass moments of their lives, or the I got screwed moments. They either fill their heads with nostalgic reminiscences of past loves, dreams, and delusions of what might have been, or with resentful feelings towards anyone, or anything, they wish to blame for past failures, problems, or personal unhappiness.

On the B-side of the same record, many people also dwell on their future, as though that were a portion of time that they were guaranteed to experience. The basic assumption of future time is pompous and inauspicious at its core. Ask anyone who has ever been blindsided by an unexpected death, or disaster, about the futility of making future plans. I mean, weren't the passengers and crew of the *S.S. Minnow* only planning on a three-hour tour?

The very idea of trying to relive the past, or pre-live the future, is a complete waste of what precious little time God gifts us. Even though I can choose to live in the past or the future, what I can't do is act in either of those time periods; I can only act in the timelessness of the present moment. That said, my actions in the present can certainly help to mend some of life's past hurts, and also help to pave the way to a better future. That much I have learned in recovery.

But, like recovery, the first step is always acceptance. I must be able to accept the present moment, whatever it is, before I am able to act in that moment. Many people have a difficult time accepting their present - which is why it is easier for them to live in the comfort of their past experiences, or their future dreams. Both of those options are illusory and nonproductive; they are dead ends.

Eckhart Tolle, author of *The Power of Now* (1999), acknowledges that sometimes the present moment (the Now) can be painful, or unpleasant. Since the egoic mind cannot function or remain in control without time (i.e. the past and future), it perceives timelessness (i.e. the Now) as threatening. It resists and is nonaccepting of what *is*. Therefore, the mind has a built-in resistance to life's present difficulties, which is why it likes to default to the past and future. According to Tolle, the more accepting we are of the Now, the freer we are of pain, suffering, and the egoic mind. Most importantly, we are free to act:

> *Accept – then act. Whatever the present moment contains, accept it as if you had chosen it. Always work with it, not against it. Make it your friend and ally, not your enemy. This will miraculously transform your whole life.*[28]

It has mine.

Daily Thanksgiving

'Twas the day before Thanksgiving, when it suddenly hit me: every day should be a day of thanksgiving, not just the fourth Thursday in November. Most people would probably agree with that observation, but how many would say that they perform the act of daily thanksgiving? I try to, but that is only a recent development. For far too many years, giving thanks to God was something I only thought about once a year, like New Year resolutions, and Birthday wishes.

We have a tradition in our home, at Thanksgiving Day dinner, of going around the dining room table, one person at a time, and verbally sharing what we are most grateful for on that particular Thanksgiving Day. Some years ago, on a Wednesday morning, while sitting in my library, considering what I might want to share at the following evening's Thanksgiving dinner, I suddenly realized how much I had to be grateful for at that present moment, on that Wednesday morning. As I sat at my desk, I was inexplicably overwhelmed with a deep sense of gratitude. I felt grateful for the beautiful autumn colors of the leaves on the trees outside my window, grateful for the warmth inside the room in which I sat, and most grateful for the fact that I was home, and that the house resonated with the sounds of my family, and the smells of baking emanating from the kitchen.

As I continued counting my blessings, I realized what a sacrilege it would be for me to take for granted, even if for only a moment, my good health, my sobriety, or the love and support of my family and friends. I recognized how sinful it would be if I didn't take the time to thank God for every minute that I get to spend holding my grandchildren in my arms, knowing how close I came to dying from the Stage-4 Hodgkin's Disease that I battled over 20 years ago.

My first experience with alcohol was on Thanksgiving Day, 1968. I was 15 years old, drank the better part of a bottle of Boone's Farm Apple Wine, and threw up my Thanksgiving dinner at my cousin's flat in Detroit. Exactly 41 years later, on Thanksgiving Day, 2009, my eldest son succinctly identified for me the root of my underlying problem, a problem shared by most alcoholics: selfishness. Being an alcoholic, and living in denial of that fact, I had no idea what he was talking about at the time. Not until I began my recovery program, 7 months later, did I understand what a gift my son had given me on that Thanksgiving. He had opened a door of revelation to me that has changed my life forever. On the following Thanksgiving, at the dining room table, as we took turns sharing what we were most thankful for, I had the opportunity to thank my son for his gift of enlightenment.

Since becoming sober, I have made a daily practice of getting on my knees, twice a day, to thank God for the many blessings in my life. I have tried to make the act of thanksgiving a daily exercise instead of an annual tradition. Only in sobriety have I come to understand, and appreciate, the difference.

Goal Setting

Anyone who has ever set personal and/or business goals knows that they are useless unless written down. Furthermore, set goals are only achieved when they are broken down into daily "to do" lists, and checked off when accomplished. Lastly, set goals must be very specific, measurable, and time-keyed. There, I've just distilled for you, in less than 50 words, everything I have ever learned about goal setting and time management from a multitude of best-selling books, and motivational seminars I have attended over several decades. You're welcome.

For those of you who, like me, have suffered from the self-paralyzing condition known as *procrastination,* the simple mention of goal setting is traumatic to our systems because we've never been successful at following through with our goals. We know how easy it is to let life get in the way of our life goals – how ironic is that? Given any opportunity to put off a personal or business goal, we'll find it, and we'll come up with the most creative excuses our little procrastinating minds can come up with. Does "my dog ate my homework" sound familiar? It's every procrastinator's credo.

I guess it's fairly accurate to admit that, for over four decades, I have used a variation of that classic line to explain why I never completed the several novels, and countless other writing projects, which I always started in earnest but, over time, put aside for another day ("The dog ate my manuscript"). What a self-created curse, this thing called procrastination. It strips us of our self-confidence, and wreaks havoc on our ability to meet homework deadlines in school, and work assignments at the office. Belated birthday cards are what we send to our friends, and last minute banal Christmas gifts are what we give to those we love. But the greatest sin of all is the precious, God-given time we waste by not doing what we know in our hearts we should be doing. But there is hope.

The transformational shift that I experienced was the moment when I realized that writing novels was something I really only *wanted* to do – for me. In fact, I often said that I would have been happy just to finish a manuscript, even if it spent the rest of eternity stored in my footlocker where I kept my writings. For me, personally, writing novels was just a way for me to release the stories that I held inside, merely a means to gift birth to these children of my creativity, even if it meant never sharing them with the rest of the world. Perhaps that is the one main reason why I was never thoroughly committed to completing any of my novels. I never felt it was something I *needed* to do, or *had* to do.

The moment I felt *called* to write *The Pono Principle,* I knew I had to write it and complete it – primarily because of its potential to help me, others, and the world in which we live. In truth, it was pono that I write this book about pono. The mutually beneficial subject matter of this book, doing the right thing in all things (i.e. pono), was too important for me not to get excited about and to dedicate myself to fully. I knew that I was being spiritually guided to write this book, on this subject, and to see it through to fruition. Obviously, I have succeeded in this task, and this completed printed book is the fruit of my labor.

Pono Power

If there was a secret to what it was about this book that motivated me to forge through the daily task of writing it, versus the years I spent starting new writing projects without completing them, it was something I will call *pono power*. What I did was modify the way I approached my daily "to do" list. As stated earlier, the more specific you make each goal, the better chance you have of accomplishing that goal. There is no sense of urgency, and very little accountability, if I write down a very imprecise goal on my daily "to do" list. But that is what habitual procrastinators will do, very much on purpose. I had to confront that, acknowledge what I had been doing, and completely change the way I set my goals - especially in the writing of this book.

The first thing I did was to stop using the term "to do" list. From now on, my goals were to be boldly written, in capital letters, under the banner MY DAILY "MUST DO" LIST. Said list has nine daily goals written on it, each one beginning with the first letter of the acronym PONOPOWER. These goals are sacrosanct and non-negotiable. No matter what, they MUST be done each and every day of my life. I will share them with you:

MY DAILY "MUST DO" LIST

- **P**RACTICE PONO IN ALL THINGS
- **O**PEN YOUR EARS TO GOD'S WHISPER
- **N**OURISH YOUR MIND, BODY, AND SOUL
- **O**BSERVE NATURE'S WONDER
- **P**RAISE THE GOOD IN OTHERS
- **O**VERCOME ALL OF YOUR ADDICTIONS
- **W**RITE, AT LEAST, 500 WORDS
- **E**XERCISE FOR, AT LEAST, 1 HOUR
- **R**EAD FOR, AT LEAST, 1 HOUR

I keep a copy of this list in my bedroom, my living room, and in my library - that way it serves as a daily reminder to me wherever I am in my home. Naturally, this list has transformed, as I have, over time. It has seen several revisions, some as recent as yesterday. It was recommended to me by my dear friend (and yoga instructor) to add the words *at least* to any goal that has time or quantity attached to it. Mind you, it wasn't very long ago when my last three goals were simply listed as WRITE, EXERCISE, and READ – without any quantifiers. Believe me, it didn't take long for the procrastinator in me to rationalize that if I exercised or read for only 15 minutes, or only wrote two sentences, that I could justify checking those accomplishments off my "to do" list. Such folly.

What my yoga instructor shared with me, that I found so inspiring, is that she has completed her daily "to do" list every single day for the last five months (as of this writing). Regardless of how late she would have to stay up at night to check off her last "to do" item, she got it done. As soon as I returned from my meditation session with her, I committed myself to treating my "MUST DO" list in the same manner. Regardless of how early I need to rise in the morning, or how late I need to stay up at night, I have promised myself that these nine daily goals are always to be completed by day's end, no matter what.

Why should that be such a hard thing to accomplish? Just because I have had procrastination issues in my past, with respect to goal setting and time management, doesn't mean that I can't commit to prioritizing nine things in my daily activities that I consider sacrosanct and non-negotiable. I don't seem to have a problem with completing daily activities like brushing my teeth twice a day, taking a shower, eating three meals, reading the newspaper, doing the crossword puzzle, and drinking my apple cider vinegar and honey drink first thing in the morning. That's nine daily activities that I have steadfastly done for most of my life, without even thinking about it. Somehow I have managed to work the rest of my day around those mundane activities for an entire lifetime. How much more important is it for me, today, to make sure that these nine pono activities become my new top priorities?

A Pono Life Lesson

In classic literature, the protagonist of the story almost always experiences a transformation, but only after stepping out of his/her comfort zone. From Odysseus to Ebenezer Scrooge, main characters in literature must *leave the Shire* before they can begin the adventures that will transform them forever - so, too, in real life. For most of my life, the idea of volunteering my time and energy for anything whatsoever was foreign to me; it definitely was out of my comfort zone. I'm certainly not proud of that fact, but I share it because it is true. That changed, almost overnight, once I became clean and sober.

Alcoholics, and addicts in general, are so full of self that the mere notion of doing something for others, without some benefit to themselves, is inconceivable. But since recovery work is all about the destruction of the *false self,* while creating a newfound concern and compassionate attitude towards *others,* all of a sudden I became interested in doing volunteer work within my community. Within a few months of starting my recovery work, I quickly signed up to be a volunteer at my local hospital and at the public library, two of the best *jobs* that I was never paid to do.

It didn't take very long, in either volunteer position, for me to understand what a blessing I had come to discover. I received so much more than I ever could have expected. Much like the feeling I had after every time I attended an addiction recovery meeting, when I would walk home from working at the hospital or library I would always have a profound sense of gratitude for the opportunity to share with, and help, others. That was a powerful new feeling for me. As unexpected as it was, I recognized that I was consistently being blessed for my efforts, and getting back much more than I felt I was giving out.

How is it that some people experience the joy of volunteering at a very early age, while others take a lifetime to discover the rewards of doing for others - if in fact they ever experience it at all? How can some people be so giving without any thought of getting back anything in return?

I believe that serving others is the highest form of living pono. Nowhere is this better demonstrated than when one serves *the least, the last, and the lost.* Even though it took me 57 years to finally address my addictions, my self-centeredness, and to start serving others, I still hadn't *completely* stepped out of my comfort zone with regards to volunteering. For some reason, the idea of volunteering to feed the homeless was a bridge too far for me. I have no doubt whatsoever that that was due to my *zombie ego* that just seems to refuse to die. Could I possibly still be that arrogant and shallow of a man to view myself as somehow *better* than any other human being? Evidently so.

My church has an amazing meal program that feeds the hungry and homebound 365 days a year. For over five years, I donated money to this program but never could picture myself either working in the kitchen or volunteering to be a driver. That changed about a year ago when I heard God's whisper to *feed His lambs.* My life hasn't been the same since. I'm actually heading out the door in a little while to deliver food to the homebound in my designated area of Kihei. (*Mahalo, ke Akua,* for this opportunity and the gift of your Divine grace).

I'm not too sure how *transformed* I was when I merely donated money to this phenomenal meal program, sponsored by my church, but I can say with absolute certainty that I have felt spiritually transformed once I physically connected with the actual people we were feeding. Certainly, donating money to different worthwhile charities is an honorable and pono act. But I can now tell you from experience that there is nothing in this world more rewarding than to serve a hungry human being, or to lend an ear to one who has had no human contact for the entire day. Nothing can possibly be more pono than to give of yourself for the betterment of another.

Living Pono is a way of life that can become habitual. But for it to become a habit, one must repeat right actions continuously throughout the day. After a while, you won't even notice that you are focused on living pono. But, what you will notice, is that you are now living the life that God had always intended for you - and the world will, indeed, be a better place for your living in it.

Beans, Seeds
& Nuts

Whole
Grains

Vegetables
& Fruit

The Pono Food Pyramid

Chapter 9

Eating Pono

So, when it comes to eating healthy, it's just doing the right thing.
- Mike Ditka

Even people who have never spent any time studying nutrition know that eating too much sugar is bad for you, that too much fat can clog your arteries, and that obesity is hard on your heart and other organs of the body. As one who has been a student of nutrition for many years, I started making some serious dietary changes over 20 years ago, when I was fighting Stage 4 Hodgkin's Disease. It was the first time in my life that I really started to connect the dots between how eating an unhealthy diet was directly responsible for so much of the world's obesity, diabetes, cardiovascular diseases, cancer, and osteoporosis. It was then, in 1995, that I chose to start Eating Pono. Today, I can honestly say to you that I am healthier than at any other time in my life.

Eating Pono is conscious eating. Personally, I believe that making dietary choices is much the same as making moral choices – so much just relies on common sense. Ironically, the same people who have no problem understanding that it's wrong for them to harm other human beings won't apply the same logic to themselves when they eat foods that they know are harmful to them. After all, if it is pono to do all we can to save humanity as a whole, doesn't that include each of us, personally, as well?

I will suggest several easy steps to take so that individuals can start making healthier food choices, and experience the inherent health benefits that will result from those choices. Sometimes it may be as simple as sitting at your breakfast table, looking at a bowl of blueberries and a glazed donut, and wondering which one to eat. You'll know when *eating pono* is starting to work for you when you feel guided to eat the blueberries (since, consciously, we already know that's a healthier choice for breakfast). When you stop buying glazed donuts (or, at least, dramatically limit them in your diet), and start buying healthier food choices, that's when eating pono becomes your new healthier lifestyle.

In Buddhism, Right View is the insight that helps us identify what makes us suffer, and what we need to do to transform from that suffering. What we choose to eat and drink, oftentimes, is responsible for our suffering. In order to maintain a healthy body, we must practice daily mindfulness. Buddhists believe that, in order to know the difference between what is healthy and what is harmful to our bodies, we need to practice Right View whenever we grocery shop, prepare our food, and eat it. We need to take a good look at how we eat, what we could choose to eat and, perhaps, most importantly, at what we could choose *not* to eat. Another practice of the Noble Eightfold Path is Right Action. With regards to what we eat and drink, it means being mindful that the majority of foods we choose to consume are healthy and safe for our bodies, our families, and our environment. Of course, this Buddhist practice is the very definition of the word Pono, and *The Pono Principle* is the best way to a healthier eating consciousness.

What's in Your Refrigerator and Pantry?

I have seen several television shows where weight loss coaches come into their clients' homes and basically raid their refrigerators and pantries, usually tossing out 99% of what they find there. As the nutritional experts are throwing all of this food away, they will usually stop and point out to their clients the ingredients of some of the foods being disposed of. Nothing is more entertaining than seeing the expressions on peoples faces the first time that they are read the nutrition facts on a box of their favorite rainbow-colored breakfast cereal, or a can of processed cheese spread. What's not funny is the realization that there are far too many American households where these foods are everyday staples consumed by families that are nutritionally uninformed and who, consequently, suffer from dietary problems like obesity and diabetes.

Unfortunately, nowhere in our country do we see this problem better illustrated than in my home State of Hawaii. According to the 2013 Hawaii State Department of Health's *Physical Activity and Nutrition Plan*, *"In Hawai'i, and the rest of the United States, there is a lack of physical activity and healthy eating practices among the majority of adults, adolescents, and children."* Based on their 2011 research statistics, the Hawaii DOH came to these shocking conclusions:

- More than 76% of adults in Hawaii did not meet the recommended guidelines for physical activity.
- More than 75% of Hawaii high school students, and 80% of middle school students, did not get the recommended amount of physical activity for youth (60 or more minutes per day).
- Nearly 81% of adults, and nearly 83% of teens, ate fewer than five fruits and/or vegetables a day (the recommended amounts are 5-9 servings a day).
- Almost 22% of Hawaii adults were considered obese and only 40% had a healthy body weight. Most shockingly, Native Hawaiians and Other Pacific Islanders had the highest obesity rate at nearly 41%.

Although Hawaii consistently ranks among the healthiest states in America, a 2014 study by the Centers for Disease Control and Prevention found that Native Hawaiians — descendants of Hawaii's original Polynesian settlers — are in worse health than many other Americans. Compared to all other ethic groups in the nation, they have the highest mortality rate from cardiovascular disease, stroke, diabetes and cancer. One of the most tragic realities facing Native Hawaiians is that their life expectancy is 6.2 years lower than the state average of all ethnic groups in Hawaii, and also among the shortest in the United States. With regards to the highest prevalence of obesity in the country, Native Hawaiians rank second only to that of Samoans.

History suggests that, prior to western contact, Native Hawaiians were generally much healthier and had little cardiovascular disease or obesity. The influence of the western diet (i.e. foods higher in fat and cholesterol, and lower in fiber) may be the biggest contributing factor to the sharp decline in the health of Hawaiians. Changing the way Native Hawaiians ate, from centuries of only eating indigenous foods from the ocean and the land, to the post-WWII years of eating Spam out of a can, is the major cause of their modern-day experiences with diseases and poor health.

Of course, there is absolutely no reason, whatsoever, why these same modern-day Native Hawaiians can't return to the healthier lifestyle of their ancestors. Just because western culture introduced processed foods and fast-food restaurants to the island chain over 60 years ago, doesn't mean that locals need to keep choosing those foods for their families diet. Of course, this same argument can be made throughout the rest of America, and the rest of the world. We all need to return to eating pono again.

Let's get back to our cleaned out kitchen.

Empowering Your Pantry With Pono Food

I'm assuming that, after getting rid of all the unhealthy food in our kitchen, we are now standing in front of an empty fridge and pantry. Good. Here is where we start to have fun, and begin to create a whole new empowering feeling about how and what we eat. Even with a very limited knowledge of nutrition, most people at least have a pretty good idea of what's not healthy to eat. That would be all the stuff you just bagged up and donated to the local food bank, or just threw out. You won't be buying that stuff anymore.

As for the pono food that we will be filling our fridges and pantries with, don't think that you need to buy several books on nutrition just to get started (although that's certainly not a bad idea). Simply start by changing the way you have bought food in the past. With very few exceptions, there is hardly any food that I can think of that I would want in my pantry that comes in a can - certainly not canned meat (sorry, all my island ohana). I was almost tempted to buy some canned soup the other day when I realized how very easy, and so much healthier, it would be to make the same soup from scratch, using fresh organic ingredients.

Canned food staples are only about one thing – convenience. They have absolutely nothing to do with healthy, nutritional eating. Before you toss all of those canned goods away, the ones that used to be in your pantry, do yourself a favor and read the nutritional labels on them. Look at the list of artificial ingredients and preservatives. Look at how much sodium and sugar are contained in the product, and what that adds to the calorie count of an individual serving. Whether it's a can of pork and beans, or spaghetti in a can, get it out of your home pronto, and begin to feel the excitement of filling your kitchen with only fresh pono food.

Farmers' Markets – A Great First Choice

Fresh is the operative word here. In my early 20s, I lived in the south of France. Oftentimes, in the morning, I would watch the locals at the food and flower market in Old Nice pick out what they were going to eat over the next several days. They would converse with the small local farmers while selecting locally produced fruits and vegetables, herbs, meats, cheeses, breads, and oils. All of the farmers' produce was fresh, as were the flowers that the locals brought home for their vases. In other words, *fresh* is what these

French locals chose to eat, and buying fresh food in the open-air market was not only their preferred way to shop - it was also a very enjoyable and healthy way of life for them.

Today, I live on Maui, almost 8,000 miles from the French Riviera. Yet, here on Maui, I have nine farmers' markets to choose from where I can buy locally produced foods, from local farmers, just like I did in Nice 40 years ago. By shopping at the local farmers' markets, I have come to know, and befriend, many produce growers, bakers, and food artisans – something I would never have enjoyed if I only purchased grocery store food.

Health Food Stores – A Great Second Choice

In almost any corner of the world today, you can find at least one health food store dedicated to specializing in nutritional, organic food. In each of Maui's most populated districts, as relatively small as they are, we have a plethora of quality health food stores available. Whether I decide to drive over to west Maui for the day, or upcountry through Paia, or just make a run into central Maui, I almost always stop at my favorite health food store to either grab a bite to eat or to do some grocery shopping. Unlike shopping in the traditional chain stores, there is something very special about buying healthy food in a friendly mom-and-pop type of environment where you feel a kindred spirit among your fellow shoppers.

Assuming that you are dedicated to filling your pantry and fridge with only the most pono (i.e. the healthiest) of foods, then you will find yourself in the Garden of Eden when you shop in your local health food store. Trust me, you will only find it foreign to you the first several times you shop there. Afterwards, you will look forward to shopping in these healthy oases. Don't be surprised if you end up recognizing many of the shoppers' faces from your visits to your local farmers' market. You will soon discover that healthy eaters are an incestuous bunch, and that's a good thing. Whatever past roads they have taken through the gauntlet of fast food chains, and unhealthy eating habits, their journeys, like yours, have eventually brought them here – to Aisle 3 of a health food store where their biggest decision of the day will be whether to buy organic rolled oats or organic oat groats.

No health food store where you live? No problem. Most chain grocery stores carry a wide selection of healthy foods. Over the past several years, my local Safeway has dramatically increased its organic produce section, and there are even times when I can find, for example, organic berries or bulk raw nuts there, when they are not available at my local health food store. Most chain stores have paid close attention to today's consumer interest in buying healthier foods and organic vegetables and fruits. That said, I still prefer to give as much of my business to the local health food store whenever possible. It just feels more pono to do so.

How to Navigate Restaurant Menus

It never ceases to amaze me how many people assume that they can't eat pono in most restaurants unless they always order a salad. Nonsense. Take it from someone who knows quite a bit about dining. In addition to the other addictions I have admitted to having throughout this book, you can feel free to add dining to that list. I have always loved the vibe that restaurants put out. Perhaps that explains why I spent the majority of my life in the restaurant business, from washing dishes in my mother's restaurant in Colorado, to being the sole proprietor of a charming European café in California. All I know is, when the restaurant bug bites you, it usually lasts a lifetime.

As someone who eats outs several times a week, while being dedicated to eating pono, I pay a lot of attention to restaurant menus and what is offered on them. Over the years, I have learned how to navigate restaurant menus so as to always be able to zero in on the healthiest choices on them. It's not exactly rocket science, but it is easy for the novice to order something perceivably healthy (e.g. fish tacos) only to discover that, because the restaurant you are eating at decided to deep fry the fish in a beer-batter, you have just ordered a meal with an entire day's recommended allowance of calorie intake, nearly two day's of salt intake, and three day's of fat intake.

This is where a little common sense can play a big part in not allowing that to happen to you. Most people have enough food savvy to know that anything deep-fried is not the best choice (in truth, it's probably the worst). Most people also know that a cream sauce on your pasta (think fettuccine alfredo) is going to be much higher in calories, fat, and cholesterol than a tomato sauce (think fettuccine pomodoro). Whole grain bread instead of white bread. Iced tea instead of a soft drink (even diet). These are what I would call common sense examples of healthier food choices that I would hope most people share.

Another key to successfully navigating a restaurant menu for healthier choices is to look for simple preparations of dishes. One of my favorite restaurant salads is a simple mix of field greens, tomatoes and fresh herbs, with a very light vinaigrette dressing. Not only is it a quick and easy salad to prepare, but the flavor is amazing and the calories are minimal. If a restaurant offers a simple healthy salad, or vegetable soup, I will always make that my first course. Since I don't eat meat, I will usually order a vegetarian pasta, pizza, or sandwich as an entrée, perhaps with some grilled vegetables as a side dish. Again, the simpler the preparation, the better (and healthier).

When I am not dining in restaurants, this is the salad I make for myself at home several times a week. I hope that you enjoy it.

Papa Lopaka's Ānuenue (Rainbow) Salad

- Plateful Organic Mixed Greens
- Handful Organic Baby Carrots
- Handful Organic Cherry Tomatoes

- ½ Organic Avocado
- Handful Organic Blueberries
- Handful Organic Goji Berries
- Handful Organic Raw Walnuts
- 2 Tsp. Organic Chia Seeds
- 2 Tsp. Nori Komi Furikake
- 2 Tbsp. Bragg Organic Hawaiian Dressing

(478 calories)

A Great Non-Vegan Business Model – Pono Burger

Not long ago, I visited my youngest son in Los Angeles where I discovered a wonderful Hawaiian-inspired restaurant in Santa Monica named (can you believe it?) Pono Burger. Owned by Chef Makani Carzino, a native of the Big Island, this is the type of restaurant I wish I had modeled years ago when I was in the business. Although I am vegan today (or vegan*ish,* as my wife insists I call myself), I accept the reality that the vast majority of the world isn't. Therefore, instead of highlighting my favorite vegan/vegetarian restaurant as the *ultimate* business model, I chose Pono Burger because it represents a huge step in the right (Pono) direction when it comes to America's most popular dining experience – the burger joint.

Chef Makani offers one of the best definitions of pono I have ever heard: "Pono, in Hawaiian, is to do things with love, to do things with integrity, to do things right." Three of my favorite words in the world – *love, integrity,* and *right* – all in one definition, used to describe the subject matter of this book, pono.

The food at Pono Burger is 100% organic, local, and made from scratch. Because I am vegan (sorry, veganish), I ordered the organic, balsamic-infused Portobello Mushroom Sandwich, with Sweet Potato Fries. My carnivore son ordered the organic, grass-fed Paniolo Burger, which seemed to stand about six inches tall. Both of us seriously thought for a moment that we had died and gone to heaven, such was our enjoyment of our lunch that day.

Painted on a corner wall in the restaurant are these words, perhaps the best summation of what I feel about Eating Pono:

PONO IS HAWAIIAN FOR
Doing Things The Right Way

Food is not a commodity, it's a relationship. What we take into our bodies becomes part of us. That's why we source our ingredients from small, local family farms, that care deeply about the quality of their products and the impact of their methods on our environment. Mahalo, Chef Makani

This is *The Pono Principle* in its truest form – where we are doing what is right for *our bodies, our family farms,* and *our environment –* the ultimate win-win-win that true pono manifests.

A Great Vegan Business Model - Crossroads

A few days after eating at Pono Burger, I took my son (and his girlfriend) to one of the most heralded restaurants in Los Angeles - Crossroads. I had read amazing things about the food at Crossroads, along with glowing kudos for its owner, Chef Tal Ronnen. The food is some of the best to be found anywhere in town – oh, and by the way, it's 100% vegan. That seems to be the way Chef Tal wishes to market his establishment, by minimizing the emphasis on *vegan,* and playing up the wonderful flavors of his beautifully presented food. As an ex-restaurateur, myself, I completely understand that strategy. It's the kind of establishment that you can take your carnivore son to (as I did), and just not tell him that the *Seafood* Tower we just ordered is 100% seafood-free. What tasted like seafood were artistically prepared artichoke oyster mushrooms *Rockefeller,* smoked-carrot *lox* with kelp *caviar,* and sustainably sourced hearts of palm *calamari,* just to name a few of the delightful offerings.

Chef Tal describes Crossroads as "an intersection where vegans, flexitarian's, omnivores and meat eaters can cross paths to share a delicious meal and a good time. There are no obvious vegan cues and most guests don't even make the connection that the menus is plant-based - they just know that the restaurant is comfortable and the food is satisfying and delicious. Crossroads is defined not by what's missing but by what it is." As someone who loves exquisitely prepared food, while consciously trying to eat pono whenever I do go out to eat, I can't think of a better fine dining experience than Crossroads. It's everything this *veganish* gourmand could ever dream of.

A Pono Life Lesson

A while ago, I had the pleasure of staying two nights in a bed and breakfast that used to be a 1924 plantation-era home, upcountry in Makawao. My major intent was to immerse myself in my writing and to also catch up on my reading. Of course, these are two very worthwhile, honorable, and right actions to take when a writer is simply trying to change his surroundings while still staying productive. Many writers take writing retreats in the midst of a project that they are working on, if only be break up the monotony of always writing at the same desk, in the same room, etc. As for my major intent, I was satisfied that it was the pono thing to do.

But then there was this minor intent I had with regards to going to Makawao. You see, there happens to be a 100-year-old bakery in Makawao that makes the best malasadas (Portuguese donuts without the hole) and cream puffs on Maui. As mentioned in the earlier chapter on addiction recovery, I suffer from a handful of addictions, one of which is food. I have an incredible sweet tooth that loves all things sugary. As a child, I worked at my Mom's ice cream parlor, and ate more penny candy than I sold from the counter. When I had children of my own, I always looked forward to taking them to the county fair just so I could have my annual binge of cotton candy, funnel cakes, and elephant ears. If it had sugar sprinkled on it, I was in. Such is my sugar addiction, and why I mention my secondary intent for wanting to go up to Makawao for a few days.

If someone recognizes that they have an addiction to food, or sugar, shouldn't they combat that addiction as seriously as they would their alcohol or drug addiction? If I am aware of the fact that I can no more eat just one donut than I can just drink one glass of wine, why would I go out and buy a dozen donuts? Why not buy a case of wine while I'm at it? How is my desire or ability to overcome one addiction any different than the other? Why should it be different? The bottom line is that neither of these addictions is good for me – neither represent pono.

So, here I am on a self-imposed writer's retreat in Makawao, working on a book about practicing pono in all areas of our lives, including how to eat well, and I am standing at the front door of this famous upcountry bakery at 7am (when they open), anxious to get my hands on those tempting malasadas and cream puffs. By the way, those words are pluralized for good reason – I don't know how to order just one malasada or cream puff when the pastry shelves at 7am are full. Which is why I am there when the bakery opens; within 2-3 hours those shelves will be completely empty.

Only an addict would go out of his way to be there when the bakery's doors open just so I would not miss out on any of the pastry selections offered there. And only an addict like myself would buy, not one, but a half dozen malasadas and cream puffs to take back to the bed and breakfast. Oh, and not to forget some donuts-on-a-stick and a coconut pie to go with that order. (I'm getting sick all over again just reading this). Although I did plan on sharing what I was purchasing with an Australian couple, who were also staying at the bed and breakfast, my heart wasn't all that broken when they informed me later that they don't usually "eat this sort of thing for breakfast."

Truth be told, after departing Makawao and driving home to south Maui, I did have a moment of clarity when I realized that I had just had a food addiction *relapse* – and so I threw the coconut pie, and remaining pastries, into the garbage can the moment I got home. The good news is that, although tempted several times, I have only had one other junk food relapse since that day in Makawao, involving a phenomenal gourmet donut shop in Wailuku. The major difference is that, although I ordered a half dozen donuts to take home, my intent was not to consume all six donuts but to merely sample each unique type in order to critique them. Although I didn't adversely increase my sugar levels or cholesterol too much by simply sampling these delicious donuts, I did learn that caving in to food addictions, of any type, is counterproductive to eating pono and, therefore, better avoided as much as humanly possible.

Of the many truths I have learned in addiction recovery, the one that I have to remind myself of daily is that *progress* is the goal, not *perfection*. When I do fall from time to time, as I know I will, I can still choose to get up, learn my lesson, and go on to do the next right thing.

Which probably has nothing to do with eating a donut.

Be Mindful

Be Joyful

Be Peaceful

The Secret

Chapter 10

Being Pono

I am in the right place at the right time, doing the right thing. All is well in my world.

- Louise Hay

At the end of the day, what everyone hopefully aspires to is to become the best person they can be. Mahatma Gandhi once said,

> *We but mirror the world. All the tendencies present in the outer world are to be found in the world of our body. If we could change ourselves, the tendencies in the world would also change. As a man changes his own nature, so does the attitude of the world change towards him. This is the divine mystery supreme. A wonderful thing it is and the source of our happiness. We need not wait to see what others do.*[29]

I believe that Being Pono is that *change,* that *wonderful thing* that Gandhi is talking about. It is, in fact, *the divine mystery supreme* when our actions are centered on doing the right thing. How could it not be? What, if anything, would constitute a higher calling? Being Pono is what the saints aspired to, it is what summons the best in each of us, and it fully defines the heroes of history, from George Washington to Rosa Parks.

Mindfulness is the First Step

The idea of Being Pono begins with mindfulness, the Buddhist idea that we must learn how to capture the beauty, wonder, or life lesson, that we are experiencing in the present moment, and not be distracted by comparatively unimportant thoughts or actions. In today's world of people proudly proclaiming what great multi-taskers they are, we have lost our ability to stop and smell the roses (i.e. entirely focused on those roses and on nothing else).

A very young, but spiritually mature, friend of mine gave me a remarkable book some years ago, *Peace is Every Step: The Path of Mindfulness in Everyday Life* (1991) by Zen master Thich Nhat Hanh. In this beautifully written book, the author suggests ways for modern-day people to find peace in the midst of the chaos of everyday life. Before he suggests different ways of increasing our mind/body awareness (by being conscious of, and practicing, a variety of breathing techniques), Thich Nhat Hanh begins his book my discussing how he starts his day, everyday, with a smile.

According to the Zen master, a smile denotes *an awakened mind* in a person, and brings happiness to both the person and to those around him or her. Of course, knowing human nature, he suggests several ways that we might remind ourselves to smile upon awaking in the morning. Keeping something that brings a smile to our face, close to our bed, is the author's suggested method. Personally, I have a little angel ornament that hangs from my ceiling fan, right above my bed, that always brings a smile to my face when I wake up. I call her my hula angel because, whenever the fan is on, the angel sways on the pull chain as though she's hula dancing. Another very young, and loving, friend of mine gave me the little angel as a gift. The words *Friendship Happiness Love* are inscribed below the angel's body, a reminder of not only the warm sentiment behind the gift but also of the pono I should be spreading throughout the world.

Of course, mindfulness is all about living in the present moment.

Thich Nhat Hanh shares another example in his book about a group of children who were offered a tangerine to mediate on. They were invited to consider the source of the tangerine, where it was grown, who was responsible for its growth, who picked it, and who delivered it to its present location. Then they were asked to slowly peel the tangerine and experience its fragrance, texture, and taste. According to the author, "You can see everything in the universe in one tangerine."[30]

I mention this particular anecdote only because I recently had a similar experience with a navel orange (which I now have growing at my home). Unlike most other times, when I would eat something while focusing on other things around me, the sweet juiciness of this one particular navel orange demanded my undivided attention. I found myself, in that moment of eating that orange, a singular mindfulness I have rarely experienced before. Like the group of children meditating on their tangerines, I was completely captivated by what I was mindful of – this navel orange. I was like Tony when he first catches sight of Maria, in the gym, in the movie *West Side Story*. I could no longer hear the background sounds of music or other peoples' conversations. I had no other distracting thoughts in my head – I was completely mindful. Everything in my *mind* was *full* of this orange.

So it is with Being Pono. When we can focus our thoughts and actions on the singular desire to do the next right thing, instead of trying to juggle a multitude of less important tasks, we are then being mindful of pono. When we put wheels in motion to start our day off with a smile (by hanging an angel ornament over your bed, for example), we are beginning our day on the right foot. When we fall to our knees to thank God for this glorious day, and for our smile, we are demonstrating gratitude and humility by keeping ourselves *right-sized*. And when we go for our morning walk, sharing our smile with others, we are doing nothing less than uplifting the world.

What's the Alternative?

I have always found it quite interesting when someone asks me a question about why I am doing something that I consider to be pono. I'll offer up two examples of what I mean. On more than one occasion I have had friends ask me, "How do you maintain such a positive attitude all of the time?" Another question I have gotten a lot since becoming sober in 2010 is, "Don't you ever miss drinking alcohol?" To both of these questions, I have a common response, "What's the alternative?" Should I choose to have a negative attitude from time to time, just to appear more *normal?* Should I allow the thought of drinking alcohol enter my brain when I know how terribly destructive it is for me?

You see, one of the realities of practicing *The Pono Principle* is that you may find yourself standing out in a crowd of others who don't understand that having a positive attitude most of the time is a choice, just like putting a plug in the jug is for a recovering alcoholic. The art of being pono is to make right decisions throughout the day, regardless of how others will judge you for those decisions. Ironically, the very friends who don't understand how someone can have such a Pollyanna attitude most of the time are the very ones who end up being the ultimate beneficiaries of that positive and uplifting attitude. Without question, I am a much better man, husband, father, grandfather, and friend because of my choice to not drink anymore - and the alternative to that choice is unthinkable to me.

And so it is with the constant self-questioning that one does throughout one's day. Could I choose to eat a healthy breakfast of fruit or oatmeal instead of the alternative glazed donut? Could I share my smile with others on my morning walk, and say "good morning" to passersby - or choose to disengage from others by putting my ear buds in my ears, and not making eye contact with those I walk by? When the alternatives are no longer attractive to you, or conflict with your sense of what is best for you and others, you know that you are making the right choice - and each and every one of those choices will compound for you as you become a person of pono.

This compounding element of pono is the unconscious enlightenment that develops just by the steady repetition of thinking about what the next right thing is that I could be doing, and what the alternative will be if I don't. As Aristotle so clearly puts it in the *Nicomachean Ethics*, "Excellence of character comes into being as a consequence of habit, on account of which it even gets its name by a small inflection from habit."[31] (In Greek, the word "character" is *êthos* and the word "habit" is *ethos).*

From "Doing" Pono to "Being" Pono

One morning, as I was reading Anne Bérubé's *Be Feel Think Do* (2017), I was struck by her observation concerning how many of us usually start our mornings by carrying over "the same old stuff" from the day before: "We quickly establish the right things to do that day to support all the thoughts and goals."[32] But in the very next chapter, she explains that for individuals to transform from *thinking* and *doing,* to *being* and *feeling,* the process may be overwhelming: "When we stop and attempt to simply be or feel for the first time in a long time, or maybe for the first time ever, it can be very difficult to trust that it is the right thing to do."[33] The metamorphosis of changing from someone who has always been a *think*er and a *do*er – to a person more in touch with their True Self inside - is truly life changing.

Of course, there are habits that we will need to change entirely. Imagine, if you will, the magnitude of self-discipline necessary for the alcoholic who has spent years orchestrating every day around his drinking habit, but who has now made the conscious decision to quit drinking. Or the reluctant husband who has spent years refusing to go to marriage counseling with his wife, but is now accepting that his marriage will have no future chance of success if he doesn't start immediately. When we deeply, and knowingly *feel* that our past habits are wrong for us, and deadly to our relationships with others, we have no real choice but to create new positive habits that will lead us to a place of happiness, and a place of pono. As my yoga instructor, Meenakshi Angel Honig, is fond of saying, "First you form your habits; then your habits form you."

But, as someone who has personally succeeded at putting a plug in the jug after 41 years of drinking, I can attest to the fact that my new habit of *not* drinking is far more powerful than my old habit of alcohol consumption. Some months ago, I celebrated my seventh year of recovery and I can honestly say that, during these past seven years, I never once had a compulsion to drink, not ever. I am not so cocky as to assume that there will never come a day when that temptation might surface again but, as of today, it has yet to be an issue. Not allowing the thought of alcohol or drug use to enter my brain is one strong example of how *The Pono Principle* works for me on a daily basis. By making pono actions my highest priorities, everyday, I have developed a new set of positive habits that have superseded most of my bad habits from my pre-recovery days.

In a previous chapter, I discuss the pono work ethic of my good friend, Ron Panzo. During my interview with him, Ron emphasized how easy and transformative it can be when focusing on doing the right thing becomes a daily habit. As fellow restaurateurs, Ron and I share the belief that the more that pono is demonstrated in the workplace, the more habit-forming it becomes. "The more you do it," he says, "the more it becomes part of you, without you being aware of it, and the easier it becomes. Once you start to do it, and you feel that 'Hey, wow, that was the right thing to do, it feels good.' And that feeling, I think, can be addicting, can be habit-forming." Certainly, I have found that to be true in every job I have ever had. The more pono that I can bring into the workplace, the better for everyone else – owners, employees, and customers.

And isn't it interesting that Ron suggests that *being* pono, and *living* pono, can become *addicting?* Which got me thinking - what if everyone became addicted to doing the right thing? What would the world be like then? What if the entire world took Robert Palmer's advice and became addicted to love? Addicted to world peace? Addicted to pono? I think I'm on to something here. We just need to turn our life-destroying addictions into life-affirming addictions, and then have at it. Binge all you want on making yourself a better person, by loving others, and working to make the world a better place for everyone. Become a pono addict today (keeping in mind that there's no letter *r* in pono).

As life-changing as it may be for a person to start focusing on doing what is right, instead of just doing *some thing,* the real transformation that takes place when one practices *The Pono Principle* on a daily basis, is when that person becomes the ideal that he or she is striving to attain. Think of the transformation (or metamorphosis) that occurs when the Scarecrow, Tin Man, and Lion in *The Wizard of Oz* acquire wisdom, emotion, and courage. Although they are rewarded for *doing* virtuous deeds - while accompanying Dorothy down the yellow brick road to The Emerald City - what they come to realize is that they were *being* these noble qualities all along.

In like fashion, who among us doesn't believe that every single child born into this world starts life as a pure *being?* I firmly believe that whatever noble qualities we seek later in life, we already possessed at birth. Why else would Jesus say, "Truly I tell you, unless you change and become like little children, you will never enter the kingdom of heaven"[34] (Matt. 18:3 NIV) unless He viewed children as the greatest among us? I feel that we misuse the term *of noble birth* when we only apply it to those born into royal families. I much prefer to use the term to describe the divine nature (i.e. soul) that is innate to every child ever born, whether that occurs in a palace or a stable. I see *nobility* less as a *birthright* of the aristocracy, and much more as a *birthmark* of a Creator God.

Since I truly believe that we come into the world as pure souls, it follows that we are imbued with a clean heart and a clear mind. I think the saddest truth concerning the human condition is that our hearts and minds, at birth, ever so slowly become corrupted and tainted over time by the influences of the world in which we live. Perhaps this is what Jesus is referring to when He is telling sinful adults that they need to "change and become like little children" again if they ever expect to go to heaven. This *change* can only occur when we are willing to completely surrender our false selves (i.e. our corrupted selves) to the trash bin, and wholeheartedly commit ourselves to finding our true selves again.

Fulfilling our Higher Purpose

Finding and fulfilling our higher (or Divine) purpose is essentially what one does when one sets out on a spiritual journey to find *one's self*. This is also the quest taken by every hero of classic literature from Odysseus to Luke Skywalker. Until we seek out, and find, our true self, that blessed individual whom God defined us to be, we are stuck with the false self of our own making. In his book *To Know Your Self* (1978), Sri Swami Satchidananda states, "Unfortunately, the moment we define ourselves – or limit the Self – we are no longer fine."[35] The true or real self is the person we must set out, not to discover, but to *re*discover. And, according to Satchidananda, it is the only way for us to know and love others:

> The aim of all spiritual practices is to know your real Self, to know the Knower. The Bible says, 'Love your neighbor as yourself.' But without knowing what your Self is, how can you love your Self in another? Know your Self and then see your own Self in your neighbor's Self. Then you can love that person as your Self.[36]

Going even deeper into the divinity of our soul, or true self, Sri Swami Satchidananda says,

When we say 'soul,' normally we mean the reflection of the Self over the mind-stuff. Soul is the spark of divinity and the image of God, while the Self is God. When you make the mind calm and serene, you realize that the soul and God are one in the same, without any distortions, without any color.[37]

I always have to remind myself that my *true* identity is described in the opening chapter of the Bible thusly, "So God created mankind in his own image, in the image of God he created them; male and female he created them"[38] (Genesis1:27 NIV).

"To be pono, or not to be pono"

Maybe Hamlet never transformed enough during the Shakespearean tragedy to ever ponder those words, but it certainly is a thought process that the rest of us face throughout the day, and throughout our lives. How many times might we feel justified to *pay back* someone because of a perceived slight? How often do we give in to the temptation to eat food that we know is not good for us? When we catch ourselves holding onto resentments towards others, do we allow them to fester in our brains rather than dismissing them the moment we discover them infiltrating our heads and hearts? These are very real life situations that all of us face on a daily basis. The simple truth is: we must choose correctly if we wish to do what is best for us, and others. And we must face the reality that only one of those two choices is the right thing to do.

The Bible tells us, "Therefore, to one who knows the right thing to do and does not do it, to him it is sin"[39] (James 4:17 NASB). The same verse, when translated in Hawaiian, uses the word pono in place of the English words *the right thing*. In other words, *not* being pono is a sin (i.e. it is an affront to God). The good news is, if we are being pono in our daily lives, we are in accord with God's wishes.

Jesus said, "It is not those who are well who need a physician, but those who are sick. I have not come to call the righteous but sinners to repentance"[40] (Luke 5:31-32 NASB). Here, when translated in Hawaiian, the word *pono* is used in place of the English words *well* and *righteous*. Jesus is basically saying that, if you are a person who practices pono in all that you do, just keep doing it. He's not concerned with your behavior because there are plenty others who choose not to be pono, and they're the ones who are in need of help and redemption.

A Pono Life Lesson

Several years ago, I was taking my early morning beachwalk. At the time, I still had a propensity for being a very prideful man (which I'm not bragging about), and when I used to walk along the beach, I had an ugly tendency to act like I was *somebody*. In typical *somebody* fashion, I would avoid eye contact with the people I passed by, had my earbuds blocking out any outside noise, and was content in my self-absorbed world of personal thought and Steely Dan music. That is, until the first day that I remember passing by a famous Maui celebrity on the beachwalk. He was walking with a beautiful young woman, and when I approached, he gave me a glorious welcoming smile and said, "Good morning."

That moment in time struck me to my core, and I paused a little further on and thought about what a self-obsessed person I had been for much of my life. When I stopped to consider that it took a well-known celebrity (a category of people that most would stereotype as socially aloof and standoffish) to teach me a lesson in humility, I began to see how self-absorbed I was. That humble gift of a sincere smile and a "good morning" from him to me was one of the purest examples of true aloha that I have been given since living on Maui.

Why do we allow the ego to create the false self that so many of us think we are? Why did I feel such a need to present myself as being a *somebody* instead of just who I am? Are we so impressed by public image and celebrity that we choose to project our false self to others in hopes to impress them? Isn't my true self also worthy of love and respect without me resorting to putting on airs and acting like a pompous so-and-so?

As a direct result of that beachwalk experience, and because of the example of humility I learned from a true bona fide celebrity, I have tried to pass on that spirit of aloha every time I walk by someone now. Today, I make it a point to make eye contact with everyone I see, and to smile and wish him or her a good day. My celebrity neighbor taught me to do that, and for that I am eternally grateful. His selfless act of aloha has caused me to do a lot of soul searching since that morning. I am now working daily on being an ambassador of aloha, and that is the truest form of pono I know.

My fervent prayer is that, together, we create an entire world of aloha ambassadors. Our planet cries out for it. Our children deserve no less. *The Pono Principle* is the way to such a world. And it starts with one simple action – just do the right thing. "What then?" you ask.

Repeat.

Afterword

Over my years on Maui, I have had the distinct pleasure, on several occasions, to meet with my fellow Wayne State University alum, Dr. Wayne Dyer. He knew my favorite English professor quite well, and it was quite enjoyable to reminisce with Wayne about Detroit in the 1960s and early '70s when we both lived there. He was truly one of the most influential people in my life, and I was so happy to have been with him at the last *Writing From Your Soul* workshop in Maui, which he spoke at, just a few months before his passing in 2015.

On his blog, Wayne once wrote that the passion within us is all we need to fulfill our dreams, and that following our passion is always the pono thing to do:

> *Passion is a feeling that tells you: This is the right thing to do. Nothing can stand in my way. It doesn't matter what anyone else says. This feeling is so good that it cannot be ignored. I'm going to follow my bliss and act upon this glorious sensation of joy.*[41]

No words could better describe what motivated me to write this book, *The Pono Principle*. As I pen these final words, I am reminded that it was my passion for the Hawaiian philosophy of pono that not only inspired me to complete this work, but, more importantly, taught me *how* to complete this work. The very last words, of the last step, in the 12-Step Program suggest that recovering addicts "practice these principles in all our affairs."[42] I am just now fully realizing how truthfully those words apply to me at this time. I could never have written this book without the constant reminder that "my bliss" is entirely dependent on how well I *walk my talk* by practicing *The Pono Principle* in every area of my life, every single day of my life. As I have honestly shared with you, in stormy weather my ship still does list from time to time, but I have a newfound clarity of purpose, *The Pono Principle,* that helps *right* the ship upon which I sail.

In like manner, I believe that Wayne Dyer was also transformed through his writings, that he embodied "this glorious sensation of joy" that he suggested his readers act upon. In the same way that writer Miguel de Cervantes is transformed into his own character, Don Quixote - in the musical *Man of La Mancha* - perhaps Wayne and I have been blessed to have these transformative words that pass through our pens become our own guiding principles. As a Maui writer, I can only hope and pray that, in some small way, I might be able to carry on where Wayne left off. Wayne loved Hawaiian culture and was very familiar with the spiritual philosophy of pono. In truth, I'm more than a little surprised that he never wrote an entire book on the subject himself.

Perhaps he left that privilege to me.

Acknowledgments

I am most grateful to the woman who walked into my life, 40 years ago, in a small Carmel wine bar, where she stole my heart (and has yet to return it). Thank you, Renee, for our life together and the loving home you created for our family. To my five children I wish to say how much of an inspiration each of you have been to me as I have watched you grow to become remarkable adults, spouses, and parents. The pride I have for you is immeasurable. To my beautiful grandchildren, to whom I dedicate the Introduction to this book, my prayer is that each of you will follow the footsteps of Kailani as you create your own wonderful world of pono.

Also, to my brother Richard, his family, and to all those deceased family members who were so instrumental in my development as a child, adolescent, and man. The example of their humble, moral lives continues to reside in the warm memories I hold dearly in my heart. They truly were the primary source of my foundational understanding of what living pono looked like when it was practiced daily.

This book would never have been written without the support, and guidance, of my addiction recovery fellowship - my sponsor, my sponsees, and all those who have so freely given to me what was so freely given to them. To my church community at St. Theresa's who taught me how to find the "secret chord that David played" in our church choir, and how to feed God's lambs through our incredible Hale Kau Kau program. God bless you all.

To the Kihei Public Library and, especially, Kathleen, for allowing "Papa Lopaka" the privilege of reading to our *keiki* the stories that I read as a little boy - when I, too, sought sanctuary in the holy temple of that little library, next to my elementary school, in Babcock Park in Hialeah, Florida. Mahalo nui loa, also, to my dearest Kailani for your many drawings, and for allowing me to witness your love of books firsthand.

I also wish to acknowledge the remainder of my Maui *ohana,* neighbors, and friends, for their continued support and aloha. To Rebecca, Sam, Angel, and the rest of our yoga "pod" at Wailea Healing Center - for your "Peace, Joy, Love and Light" – Namaste. To the "Sadhu of Keawakapu," Amon, for your friendship and spiritual guidance. To my "bruddahs" at the Grand – the Botero Boyz upstairs and the Fitness and Spa Boyz (and Girlz) downstairs – you guys are simply *'oi loa.* To Jeb, and all the other amazing restaurant owners, managers, and staff, who have supported and encouraged me, all the while reminding me of the genuine joy one receives by serving others. To Katy and Cindy – mahalo for your steadfast encouragement and kindness, and for your faith in me during my journey to publication.

I want to especially send out warmest aloha to Kimokeo and Ron for allowing me to interview them for this book. I honestly don't know of two men who better demonstrate the practice of living pono, in *everything* they do, than they. You men inspire and humble me, and, for that, I am most grateful.

Lastly, to my *bon ami,* Willie, whom I met in 1976, when we were both expatriate Americans pursuing our muse in Nice, France - he as a musician and me as a writer. Willie still lives in Nice, but has never stopped believing that I would be a published writer someday. *Merci, mon ami,* for your steadfast faith in me, a faith that, for many years, I had lost myself. Well, here it is, at last - my book! Better late than never. Let's celebrate with a pizza on the Rue de France when next I see you, *d'accord?*

Ok, I'll buy.

Endnotes

Preface

1   Pukui, Mary Kawena, and Samuel H. Elbert. *Hawaiian Dictionary.* (Honolulu: University of Hawaii Press, 1986).

Chapter One

2   Hay, Louise. *The Essential Louise Hay Collection.* (Carlsbad: Hay House Inc., 2013), 29.

3   Aristotle. *Nicomachean Ethics.* (Newburyport: Focus Publishing, 2002).

4   *The Holy Bible: New International Version.* (Grand Rapids: Zondervan, 2011).

5   Ibid.

Chapter Two

6   *The Holy Bible: New International Version.* (Grand Rapids: Zondervan, 2011).

7   Ibid.

8   Pukui, Mary Kawena, and Samuel H. Elbert. *Hawaiian Dictionary.* (Honolulu: University of Hawaii Press, 1986).

9   Satchidananda, Swami. *To Know Your Self: The Essential Teachings of Swami Satchidananda.* (Buckingham: Integral Yoga Publications, 1978), 293.

Chapter Three

10   *The Holy Bible: New International Version.* (Grand Rapids: Zondervan, 2011).

11   Ibid.

12   Shakespeare, William. *The Complete Oxford Shakespeare: Hamlet.* (New York: Oxford University Press, 1987), 1128.

13   *The Holy Bible: New International Version.* (Grand Rapids: Zondervan, 2011).

14   Satchidananda, Sri Swami. *The Golden Present: Daily Inspirational Readings.* (Buckingham: Integral Yoga Publications, 1987), June 23.

15   Satchidananda, Swami. *To Know Your Self: The Essential Teachings of Swami Satchidananda.* (Buckingham: Integral Yoga Publications, 1978), 179.

16   Ibid, 4.

17   Emerson, Ralph Waldo. *Essays and Lectures: The Over-Soul.* (New York: The Library of America, 1983), 398.

Chapter Four

18   Alcoholics Anonymous. *Alcoholics Anonymous, 4th Edition.* (New York: A.A. World Services, 2001), 59.

19   Ibid, 62.

20   Ibid, 73.

21   Ibid, 59.

22   James, William. *The Letters of William James: 2 Volumes Combined.* (New York, Cosimo Inc., 2008), 199.

23   Alcoholics Anonymous. *Alcoholics Anonymous, 4th Edition.* (New York: A.A. World Services, 2001), 76.

24   Frank, Anne. *The Diary of Anne Frank: The Revised Critical Edition.* (New York: Doubleday, 1986), 712.

Chapter Eight

25   Emerson, Ralph Waldo. *Essays and Lectures: Self-Reliance.* (New York: The Library of America, 1983), 270.

26   Ibid.

27   Longfellow, Henry Wadsworth. *Poems and Other Writings.* (New York: The Library of America, 2000), 4.

28   Tolle, Eckhart. *The Power of Now: A Guide to Spiritual Enlightenment.* (Novato:New World Library, 1999), 29.

Chapter Ten

29   Gandhi, Mahatma. *The Collected Works of Mahatma Gandhi: Vol. 12.* (Ahmedabad: Navajivan Press, 1914), 163.

30   Nhat Hanh, Thich. *Peace is Every Step: The Path of Mindfulness in Everyday Life.* (New York: Bantam Books, 1991), 22.

31 Aristotle. *Nicomachean Ethics: Book Two.* (Newburyport: Focus Publishing, 2002), 21.

32 Bérubé, Anne. *Be Feel Think Do.* (Carlsbad: Hay House, Inc., 2017), 118.

33 Ibid, 123.

34 *The Holy Bible: New International Version.* (Grand Rapids: Zondervan, 2011).

35 Satchidananda, Swami. *To Know Your Self: The Essential Teachings of Swami Satchidananda.* (Buckingham: Integral Yoga Publications, 1978), 5.

36 Ibid, 3.

37 Ibid, 4.

38 *The Holy Bible: New International Version.* (Grand Rapids: Zondervan, 2011).

39 *The Holy Bible: New American Standard Bible.* (Honolulu: Mutual Publishing, 2014).

40 Ibid.

41 Dyer, Wayne W. *Passion is Your Power.* [Blog post]. Retrieved from http//www.drwaynedyer.com, 2010.

42 Alcoholics Anonymous. *Alcoholics Anonymous, 4th Edition.* (New York: A.A. World Services, 2001), 60.

About the Author

Robert DeVinck believes that Life is the ultimate teacher, and that he is but a pilgrim student on the road to discover Life's Truth. He further believes that we serve one another by sharing the Truth we have learned from Life. *The Pono Principle* is the transformative Truth that he found on his road, and is willing to share with everyone.

DeVinck has a Masters Degree in Human Services Counseling: Life Coaching from Liberty University. He is married, has five children and six grandchildren.

He lives on the island of Maui, where he presents a Pono Workshop to other pilgrim students.